College Success Stories
That Inspire

Lessons from Inside and Outside
the Classroom

Steven Roy Goodman

Library of Congress Cataloging-in-Publication Data

Steven Roy Goodman, College Success Stories That Inspire: Lessons from Inside and Outside the Classroom; college, university, higher education, students, professors

ISBN-13:
978-1939282378

ISBN-10:
1939282373

Summary: This collection of witty, inspiring, and thought-provoking essays empowers prospective students and others eager to understand the complete college experience—lessons learned from triumph and near disaster and from professors and peers, as well as the turning points that helped launch careers and define character.

Published by Miniver Press, LLC, McLean Virginia

First edition January 2018

Table of Contents

Introduction

Over the past 20 years, I've had thousands of conversations with college-bound students and their families. One that stands out, which partly inspired this book, is a conversation I had early in my counseling career with a parent whose daughter had just been accepted to Princeton University. After all the excitement about the successful application and after thanking me repeatedly, the mother admitted in a moment of candor, "Now that _____ was admitted, there is nothing left for me to worry about!"

Actually, the college journey for her daughter was about to begin. I was excited for my student but eager to ensure that admissions success would also translate to long-range intellectual curiosity and academic growth. Happily, this was the case.

My post–Princeton acceptance conversation continues to serve as a good reminder as I begin working with new students every year. College admissions success is important, but preparing for and having a fulfilling college experience is ultimately more important.

As a college advisor and strategist, I help U.S. and international students identify schools that are a good fit or offer particular academic and extracurricular programs. Along the way, I often walk a fine line between helping a student navigate a specific field of interest and encouraging a student to explore completely new opportunities.

When should we suggest a student broaden his or her thinking? When should we encourage a student to focus on particular areas of expertise?

The stories in this book cross back and forth over this line. Some contributors are glad they participated in certain activities or studied specific things in college. Others are pleased that someone on campus challenged them to pursue fields or classes they had never considered before.

What does this mean for you, the prospective student? You have in your hands a smorgasbord of ideas, paths, and experiences that await you during your college years.

Even before you begin searching for the right schools, you can develop a nuanced understanding of various aspects of collegiate life and plan to maximize your own higher education experiences.

For parents, this book will assist you as you guide your child through the ups and downs of the college admissions process. The stories and reflections will trigger memories that can be useful today. You'll be able to look at your own college experiences in a broader context while your son or daughter learns about a wide selection of university resources.

For alumni associations and reunion committees, this book will facilitate connections between alumni of different ages and serve as the basis for meaningful group education discussions.

Back to you, the student.

While some people believe your path is predetermined, I want you to be inspired by the stories in this book and then make up your own mind about the future. Have the courage to explore what you could potentially like, consider a range of postsecondary programs, and find your own academic and extracurricular balance.

Let's go ahead and see what college experiences may await you.

Tough Choices

In the course of my counseling career, I have had hundreds of conversations with parents concerned about their students' academic progress. Imagine the consternation at the childhood home of Roy Pomerantz, then a Columbia University sophomore with an invitation to leave Columbia and prepare to join the circus. Here are the details of his story:

"Congratulations, Roy! You have been chosen to attend the most selective college in the country. From over 5,000 applicants, only 60 students have been admitted."

I was extremely excited when Dean Severini of Ringling Bros. and Barnum & Bailey Clown College calmly said those words to me over the telephone. I had completed a detailed application, auditioned twice, appeared on several television networks, and returned to Madison Square Garden for a final interview, but was still a little stunned when the call came. I also knew that I would have to make a very difficult decision.

I was being asked to indefinitely leave Columbia in order to study with the finest performers in the world and eventually tour with "The Greatest Show on Earth."

The call from the dean of Clown College forced me to seriously reflect on the progress and importance of my academic career and to consider my life's direction.

My interest in the circus originated from juggling, a skill I had become adroit at while attending high school. Three-, four-, and five-ball patterns seemed second nature to me after studying with the MacArthur "Genius" Fellow Michael Moschen at the New York School for Circus Arts. Art festivals, store openings, hospitals, trade expositions, and comedy clubs were all perfect places to demonstrate and improve my performance. I even entertained on the steps of the New York Public Library. These exposures prepared me well for my Las Vegas debut at the Sahara Hotel.

However, my love for Columbia and the education I was receiving permeated much of my thinking. At that moment, I was immersed in Columbia's Core Curriculum courses, including Literature Humanities and Contemporary Civilization. When Ringling Bros. requested the final response, my decision became obvious. I loved my Columbia classes and was actively involved with many different student organizations. I still had two years of undergraduate work to complete, and my aspiration was to become a counselor-at-law.

I promised myself I would continue to pursue object manipulation throughout my life. Clown College would have to commence without me.

My decision to reject Ringling Bros. in no way precluded my continued involvement with juggling. I became the featured entertainer in dozens of halftime shows at Columbia football and basketball games. I also taught a juggling course for the Alternative Education Program and founded the Columbia Juggling Club.

I have had a fulfilling career in law and business and on a good day can still complete a run of 100 throws with five clubs. I still juggle for numerous charitable and philanthropic organizations.

My decision to stay at Columbia enabled me to pursue a rewarding career while still keeping up with my artistic passion. But there are times I see Penn & Teller's Penn Jillette (a Clown College graduate) on television and still think it would have been fun to have had classmates like him at Clown College.

Jerome Hill, assistant to two Hollywood film producers and a 2009 graduate of Syracuse University, shares what he was afraid of and lessons he learned from his college experience:

Whenever I think about college, I almost always come to the same conclusion. I worried too much about my grades. Grades are important, of course, but allow me to explain.

I was accepted to Syracuse in the engineering school, but I had my heart set on the Newhouse School of Public Communications. Newhouse is one of the top communications schools in the United States, and my high school grades were not good enough to get me in.

On top of that, Syracuse's financial aid office said that my expected family contribution would be $10,000 per year. Did they not review my FAFSA (Free Application for Federal Student Aid)? I wrote the school a letter begging for more financial aid, promising that they would not regret helping me to attend. Eventually, I received a new financial aid package that allowed me to go to Syracuse.

But there still was the matter of getting accepted by Newhouse. I was told that I would need to get at least a 3.5 GPA in my first year at Syracuse in order to transfer into Newhouse.

No one in my family had graduated from college. How was I going to not just survive, but also excel? Nevertheless, I made it my mission to do so. After all, I wanted to get into Newhouse, and I made a promise to Syracuse University that they would not regret giving me a bigger financial aid package.

My GPA for my first year at Syracuse was a 3.7. I made it into Newhouse! Not only that, but I also received several additional university scholarships because of my high academic performance. This was amazing! I wanted to keep the momentum going.

I had been speaking with the track coach about trying out for the team, but I ended discussions because I felt that running track would interfere with my academics. Also, my Spanish professor encouraged me to consider studying abroad in Madrid. I had been excelling in class, but she felt a semester abroad could really help me become fluent.

Study abroad? Academically, I was doing quite fine in the United States. Why risk it?

There were also a bunch of amazing classes that piqued my interest: wine tasting, illustration, computer coding, Greek mythology, and several business classes. None of these were required courses for graduation. Why, I reasoned, should I take extra classes for fun, only to give myself a heavier course load and risk ruining my beautiful GPA?

In 2009, I graduated magna cum laude from the Newhouse School of Public Communications at Syracuse University with a bachelor of science in television, radio, and film. I'm very proud of this.

However, I can't help but think about all of the experiences I missed out on because of my fear. I used to lie to myself and say I was just trying to stay focused, but today I have come to terms with my college career and can admit that I was afraid.

Don't get me wrong: I had a lot of fun in college. But looking back, I could have been a Division I college athlete!

My first time traveling abroad was for 2 weeks during the holidays when I was 26 years old. I could have had Syracuse help me live in another country for 4 months!

And every day, I come up with a new idea for an app that could make me an instant billionaire. I regret not taking those coding classes. I regret not taking advantage of everything college had to offer.

One day, when I have children, I plan to tell them about my college experience. In addition to encouraging them to go to Syracuse, I'll remind them that college is meant to be a microcosm of the broader world. You must find a healthy balance between work (academics) and having enriching life experiences.

Danny Ly, a 2001 graduate of Portland State University, talks about her pre-med to community health path:

Growing up, I knew I would go to a college in Oregon. The plan was to major in pre-med and eventually apply for medical school, because that was the profession I was most exposed to from all my allergy visits to the doctor.

I visited all the major public universities in the state. Even though my parents wanted me to attend Portland State University and live at home, I fell in love with the campus of Southern Oregon University in Ashland, a 5-hour drive from Portland.

I started my college career in the fall, and with my newfound freedom, I was immediately challenged with balancing social life and homework. Homework meant spending endless hours in a lab. By the spring, I panicked, having doubts about my major. I had no backup major!

I felt I was about to disappoint my family. After all, I was the first to actually go to college. I scheduled a meeting with one of my professors. He asked me a series of thoughtful questions that really got me thinking about my chosen major. Finally, he asked me if I had ever thought about community health. Southern Oregon University did not have a robust community health program, so I decided to consider transferring to Portland State University.

In addition to my classes at Portland State University, I became civically involved in my community, which I had never paid attention to before. I spent the next 3 years volunteering at community health centers and on issue campaigns advocating for LGBT rights. I also had the opportunity to take a senior capstone course led by Gretchen Kafoury, who exposed me to issues like affordable housing and childcare. I credit her with also assisting me in landing my first job with the Oregon legislature, which was the first building block of my government relations career.

7

Stephanie Seibel graduated from Sonoma State University in 2011. She shares how she came to appreciate credentials and credibility:

A psychology professor with a specialty in East-West psychology, a branch of psychology that mixes Eastern philosophy with Western neuroscience, told me that if you want to change the world, get credentials. He explained that if you want to do bold work, you'll need credibility—and that in order to get credibility you need credentials.

I had sought advice from him multiple times, initially on academic matters, but then on the field of psychology in general, and on larger career advice. His advice was so frank yet true and was a stark contrast to the perspective I held as a 19-year-old. At the time, I was a bliss-following undergraduate who assumed passion to change the world would be enough to be successful. I knew I wanted my work to have an impact, and assumed I could simply figure it out as I went along.

My professor helped me see, however, that part of making an impact is doing your work in a manner that can be received, successful, and truly helpful to others on a large scale. In order to do that, you need a certain level of respect and trust from your audience—and having credentials is a wonderful way to gain those things.

My professor joked that because he had a Ph.D., he had the freedom to say bold things, and that he could make the changes he wished in his industry. Having a Ph.D., for instance, allowed him to bring Eastern philosophy to Western neuroscience—a concept that could be considered unusual. Were he to have made those claims in his early career, the academic community might not have listened.

There are many different ways to build credibility in the modern age, but his main point still seems to hold true and has motivated me immensely.

Margaret King directs the Center for Cultural Studies & Analysis, a think tank that studies cultural history and civilization. She shares how one of her college professors encouraged her to focus on language and observation—instead of the art that was the subject of the professor's course:

At the University of Oregon, I was fortunate to be a student of abstract impressionist painter Morris Yarowsky. This artist, who I later saw as a "painter's painter," was seriously at work on problems in modernist and post-modern theory and sensibility. He thought students should be just as involved, and so he offered one of the earlier undergraduate Art Criticism courses. Not only was I taking studio classes, but I was also offered the chance to do something adult and intellectual—something quite new and arresting.

Setting the bar at the upper levels of a discipline was exhilarating just as a trust exercise. Here was a specialized entrée to philosophy, perception, culture, and ideas—lots of them. For a junior in my new major, this offer was heady stuff. It gave my studio efforts that extra edge, showing me the faint profile of theory.

Art Crit 101 was the place students could talk about anything—high and low culture alike, to explore its interface with the arts—Pop, Op, performance, feminist, minimal, conceptual, psychedelic. We read *Art Forum* cover to cover, as a feast for the philosophical mind as well as the eager eye. I learned later that our teacher had a philosophy degree from Columbia; his core interest was clearly a Philosophy of Art.

So I was caught off-guard when my professor, having seen both my art and some starting criticism, asked to see me in his office. The term was nearly halfway through, and as far as I knew, he liked what I was doing. As a practice piece, I wrote up a blow-by-blow review of the current graduate gallery show. I wanted to know what my teacher thought, because I believed I had picked up on at least a few of his cues as leads into the critic's art.

9

"You really have a flair for language and observation," he started. I waited. "I wanted to talk with you about that." Okay, so far, so good. "Have you declared a major?" he asked. Here it comes. He's going to invite me into the art club. "Because if you haven't," he went on, "I'd like to discourage you." What? Why? Wasn't it his job to do just the opposite? To be generously, promiscuously encouraging about his own profession? "The reason I say this is that I think you're going to be a far better writer than artist."

My art wasn't bad. I had been getting Bs and a few As. What was going on?

I realized soon enough that he was doing me a favor both great and rare in steering my career off the fine arts path, where few outside an elite 1% make their living. Instead, I entered the even less-traveled career of cultural analyst (as I call what I do). But this is a profession I've created and largely control, and it's custom tailored to what I do well in my practice of 4 decades.

The Unexpected Redirection Moment forced me to look deeply at what I did and did not do best, thanks to a teacher who could identify my better talents and recommend against my expected career path—his own. It is the avowed purpose of a college education, after all, not only to foster hopes and feed dreams, but also to help students do the hard and ego-wracking work of seeing where they have the best chances of taking root and thriving. Using very few well-chosen words, Yarowsky accomplished this, and I was smart enough at the time to connect to the advice. Over the decades, we stayed in touch, and he continued to encourage my cultural work.

College, in fact, nudged me away from art to explore a Philosophy of Culture. Cultural analysis gives me art and more as human expression, thinking, and behavior across time and space, closer to the anthropology museum than the art gallery. Though I often take a turn through the shows to muse on the road not taken.

Good Advice

Samantha Auburn Levine, a 2009 graduate of Skidmore College and a 2013 graduate of Western New England School of Law, shares her law-to-jewelry path:

On an unusually warm day in late October, I walked into the Skidmore College metals studio looking for Professor Peterson. I had just left my advisor's office and needed a second opinion.

I was a senior at Skidmore and trying to decide what to do with the rest of my life. No big deal.

From the time I was 10 years old, I had adamantly decided that I was going to be an attorney. I was the president of the mock trial club in high school and had also interned for many years at a law office.

At the same time, I was also completely head over heels in love with another major field: metalsmithing. I discovered jewelry and metals during my 8th grade tour of Horace Greeley, my high school, and then ended up becoming the founder and president of the Horace Greeley Jewelry Club, as well as the metalsmithing teacher's assistant.

So back to that warm fall day in Saratoga Springs, where I was an American Studies major who was minoring in Jewelry and Metals. I was approximately 7 months away from graduation, and torn between two completely opposing futures. I had, from the beginning, always seen jewelry as a hobby. It was never meant to be a career. It was too fun to be a job. I thought that jobs had to be boring and done at a desk.

I had a meeting with my advisor, Professor Lynn, that morning to discuss my future. I told her that I had been working on my law school applications and studying for the LSAT. She was insistent that law shouldn't be my future.

Professor Lynn didn't sugarcoat things. She straight-out told me to rethink the future I had been planning for myself for almost a decade.

I was really confused. I beelined it across the green, walked by Case Center and the Library and straight into the metals studio in search of Professor Peterson. I was deathly hoping Professor Peterson could shed some light on my current predicament.

I explained the situation to him in detail. He knew most of it, as I had him as a professor for 3 years, and he had gotten to know me quite well. He looked at me and said, "Sam, you can make jewelry with a law degree, but you can't practice law with a jewelry degree." And that was it. I was wholeheartedly convinced by those eighteen words that I was going to follow the path that I had been on for 10 years and send in my law school applications.

I managed to convince myself to put my metalsmithing aside to focus on becoming a lawyer. I was accepted to law school and knew that life was going to be good as a lawyer.

At first, I enjoyed law school immensely. I found the discussions quite interesting, thought provoking, and challenging. But halfway through my first year, I found myself miserable. I missed jewelry. I missed making things and using my hands. I missed the feeling of producing a finished piece, wearing it, and showing it off. All I had were finished papers, which I couldn't exactly wear around my neck.

So I decided to sign up for some metals classes about an hour away from school. I was so happy to be back in a studio creating wearable pieces of art. I realized how much I missed it and asked my parents if they would mind a small metals studio in our house. They obliged (clearly not fully comprehending what it entailed—blow torches, late-night hammering, and loud music).

I ended up finishing law school while continuing my metals classes.

My jewelry and metals work is now my full-time career. Three years ago, I created a company called Auburn Jewelry and now produce tons of original pieces of jewelry per month. My pieces, which are mostly sterling silver and enamel, have been featured in *Seventeen* and *Hollywood Reporter*. I still work late into the night in the basement studio of our house.

I've learned that a job doesn't have to be boring or completed in an office. I wake up every day, roll out of bed, walk downstairs, and live the dream. I couldn't be happier.

Carl Ehrlich, Harvard University Class of 2009, is founder of Flag Star Football, a youth football league in Washington, D.C. In college, Carl was captain of Harvard's football team. He explains how he still uses the "just get it done" muscle that he developed during spring-ball practice:

When I think about my college sports experience, playing for and captaining the Harvard football team, it feels like a different world.

In my job, I mentor lots of current college football players and find myself sharing old stories (as we athletes tend to do) with a certain level of disbelief.

Every year, groups of players and I talk about the demands of spring-ball practice. For those who've never had the pleasure, spring ball is one of the most miserable experiences in the world. Spring-ball practice is really a series of football practices held in the spring, when there are no big scheduled games or any light at the end of the weekly tunnel.

I remember those practices as a swirl of angry coaches, loud whistles, whipping winds, bitter cold, brittle fingers, grueling drills ... you get the point.

During all of that, I remember thinking to myself things like "This is brutal" and "I can't wait to take a warm shower."

When I think about it now, and when I talk to players in the midst of spring-ball practice, I think "impossible" and "How did I survive that torture?"

The point was, and is, that college athletics threw me into a world that pushed me beyond my comfort zone. It built up my "just get it done" muscle.

While what I need to get done now looks a lot different than slamming into 300-pound men, I use that "just get it done" muscle every day of my life.

Another Harvard graduate, Ed Lazere, is Executive Director of the DC Fiscal Policy Institute. Ed talks about how the research he did as an undergraduate inspired his career:

Little did I know that taking Intro to Sociology as a college sophomore—on a whim and unrelated to anything I had studied before—would change the course of my career and life. And little did I know that the work I did for two particularly enjoyable sociology classes, using statistical analysis to study racial and economic inequality in the United States, would be something I could actually do for a career! Yet here I am, 30 years later, doing just that. I spend my workweek analyzing the economic challenges facing low-income communities in Washington, D.C., and then advocating for budget and policy changes to improve opportunities for all residents. I feel incredibly lucky to be doing work that is intellectually challenging and uses my academic strengths to make a difference.

In those two college classes, taught by Professor Roderick Harrison, we read about the lack of economic mobility in the United States—the fact that growing up poor would probably mean ending up poor as an adult. Beyond the interesting subject matter, the class was great because it took an approach that was different from any other I had taken and was very empowering. Rather than just reading theories or about research others had done,

Professor Harrison explained that questions about economic opportunity or the lack thereof were empirical issues that we could answer with our own research.

Way before the days of powerful personal computers, my fellow students and I were given access to Harvard's mainframe computer and to a rich set of economic data.

I used my research and paper assignments to challenge President Ronald Reagan's views on poverty and the safety net: that poor people don't want to work and that government programs create dependence. It didn't sound right to me, but before this class it was simply a matter of differing values.

I examined the circumstances of children who grew up in poverty, some on welfare and some in families that worked most of the time. I found that the children who grew up working poor were just as likely to end up poor as adults as were the children who grew up on welfare.

If my research was sound, I had proved that poverty was holding families back, not welfare. I felt like I had proven President Reagan wrong.

This was exhilarating in a lot of ways, so much so that I sought ways to keep doing it after I graduated. I got to decide what hypotheses I wanted to test. I got to design the research. And my research was resulting in findings that no one else had come up with before. It was original and meaningful research.

After spending a few years working with low-income students at an education nonprofit, I decided I wanted to return to research. As I gathered information on possible jobs, I would tell people about my college research and why it was exciting to me. Fortunately, several people pointed me to the universe of nonprofit research organizations— think tanks—and the ones focused on U.S. poverty. My cover letter also described that research, and it captured the eye of a few prospective employers. I landed a research internship at the Center on Budget and Policy Priorities, which quickly turned into a paying position.

Today, my organization—the DC Fiscal Policy Institute—conducts research on economic issues. We have documented the disappearance of affordable housing and growing income inequality in the city, which are now common knowledge among D.C.'s policymakers. Our research also supports other nonprofits as they advocate for things like homeless services, job training, and health care.

I am excited every week to think about the research I get to design, how it generates information that otherwise wouldn't exist, and how it makes a difference.

American University graduate Rachelle Jailer Valladares runs internship programs for study abroad students in London. She gives an orientation session every term about the value of internships:

My first internship was with a magazine called *Biblical Archaeology Review*. I did some research, but mostly I did a lot of sub-editing. I learned two very valuable lessons while interning there: (1) Biblical Archaeology was not my thing, and (2) the importance of editing.

Often the most valuable lesson you can learn from an internship is that the field you thought you wanted to go into isn't really what you want to do with the rest of your life. Better to learn that in a three-month internship than in a job that you have for years.

The other thing is that, no matter how much you don't like an internship and think it is irrelevant to your future, you will almost always learn something new from the experience. I learned to edit, a skill that I continue to use to this day.

Gwen Cummings, a 2015 graduate of the University of Oregon now working in Washington, D.C. to strengthen international nongovernmental organizations, reflects on how she ended up on her path:

The most profound moment in my college career took place on my first day of classes during my freshman year. I went to the University of Oregon unsure about my professional interests. However, I knew I had a big heart and a desire to help others, as well as a passion for adventure and a love of travel. As gratifying as these attributes are, they do not necessarily translate to a clear career path.

With a lack of any idea which classes to take and a desire to make new friends, I signed up for a Freshman Interest Group. FIGs, as we affectionately called them, expose new students to a variety of different classes and offer practical collegiate development tools. It was because of this group that I ended up in International Studies 240: Perspectives on International Development.

I did not expect much going into my first college course; I didn't have any particular academic passions in high school and rarely felt enthused by a syllabus. This time was different. The professor walked in and delivered a course introduction unlike any I had heard before.

For the next hour, he talked about the trials of developing countries, the challenges with international aid, and the power of cultural awareness and understanding. He ended our first day of the course by slamming his fist on his desk and shouting to the lecture hall, "If you aren't pissed off, you aren't listening." I was listening.

I didn't know it at the time, but that class became the touchstone to which I often return when explaining to others what led me to a career in international development.

I often think back to my 18-year-old self who felt strongly about causes but had so much to learn and to become even more passionate about. As my interest in international development advanced and my knowledge of world affairs grew, I fell more in love with the field. Now, as a young professional working in the NGO sector, I am grateful that my path was unclear when it began. It was because I explored my interests that I have ended up finding a place where I belong in an industry I feel proud to be a part of.

Jon Clemmons is Assistant General Manager for the Asheville Tourists Baseball Club. Jon earned his undergraduate degree from North Carolina State University in 2008 and his MBA from Lenoir Rhyne University's Center for Graduate Studies in Asheville in 2015:

Whether you are in an undergraduate, graduate, or work setting, being able to balance your assignments with the demands of everyday life is critical in minimizing stress levels and performing at a superior level. My undergraduate mentor and Parks, Recreation and Tourism Management professor challenged me in this area during my time at North Carolina State University. As I endure the long hours of today's Minor League Baseball industry, the more I understand the true meaning behind Dr. Jason Bocarro's wisdom of maintaining a work-life balance.

Between the months of April and September, normal days last anywhere from 12 to 16 hours. However, time usually goes by fast when I am entertaining and serving fans at McCormick Field, home of the single-A affiliate of the Colorado Rockies, the Asheville Tourists Baseball Club. I thoroughly enjoy this line of work as it intertwines my love for baseball, management, the Spanish language, and the entertainment industry into one workplace.

However, I still remember to take advantage of my time away from work and try to utilize it well. Working by day and studying in graduate school by night reinforced Dr. Bocarro's thought process because each hour, minute, and second of my day had to be optimized to the best of my ability.

I highly recommend some form of exercise or an activity that allows you to shut your brain off for at least 30 minutes every day to release stress. I enjoy running, but if playing video games or grabbing a cup of coffee with your best friend helps you decompress, then do it! Make time each day to take care of yourself mentally and physically, and I promise you will be more engaged with your work, and, as a result, be more productive with your allotment of time. Each second of the day isn't promised, so make them all count.

Evelyn Pereira, a fellow at the U.S. Food and Drug Administration and a 2014 graduate of The College of New Jersey, shares an important conversation that she had with her advisor during senior year:

As a soon-to-be first generation college student, I picked a college with a strong biology program because I knew I wanted to go to medical school.

I plan everything, from the time I wake up in the morning to each meal of the day, and I make an effort to plan and be prepared for every day.

By the looks of it, my college plan was on track because I was doing well in my classes and had great research and internship experiences.

However, the part that wasn't planned was that I would change my mind. As senior year started, I realized that I no longer wanted to go to medical school. The fact that I was doing well in my classes left me conflicted. I was interested in public health and wanted to focus on preventive approaches to health rather than treatment.

By February of senior year, I still had no plans for after graduation. Having no plans terrified me. It made me anxious. Every time professors or friends would ask about my future plans, I would laugh it off and change the subject.

With a week left in February, things finally came into perspective. I went to speak with my advisor, with whom I had a great relationship. Mrs. Cruz was the type of advisor you could tell anything to. She knew when you needed a shoulder to cry on and when you needed a reality check.

I guess she could sense something was amiss because she immediately asked me about my plans. For the first time, I truly let my emotions take over and completely broke down into tears. I told her I was confident in my decision to change my career goals, but that I felt lost in how to accomplish my new goals.

I didn't have parents who understood the process of applying to graduate school and the impact of graduate school on different jobs. In fact, they truly didn't even understand what public health really was. In their eyes, success came in the form of being a doctor, lawyer, or one of the well-known professions.

In addition, I didn't have a strong network of mentors in the science field who were helping to guide me. I had not yet taken my GRE to apply for graduate school because I didn't have the money to cover the costs, and the process to obtain a fee waiver was taking longer than expected.

On top of everything, I was upset about being newly out of a relationship and only a few days shy of my 21st birthday. As I finished crying and telling her my list of problems, I said, "I am the one who always has my life together. I am embarrassed and scared. And, frankly, I feel like a failure because I don't have my plans together by this point."

Once I finished, she gave me a puzzled glance and started to laugh. That was not the reaction I was expecting, but it definitely helped lighten up the mood in the room.

She explained that not having plans was actually a blessing in disguise and that no matter how much I plan, life will always be full of unexpected realities. We talked through each problem individually and she helped me see my problems as opportunities rather than limitations.

She encouraged me to think about being a first-generation student as a source of pride and not as a roadblock. We spoke about how I could use this unique part of my identity in personal statements for graduate school and how it could help shape my work in the public health field. We spoke about the complexity of the graduate school process and how the deadlines for Master of Public Health programs were as late as June and that I still had plenty of time to prepare applications and take my GRE.

She couldn't help me when it came to being single or planning my 21st birthday, but she made me appreciate the unique situation I was in and how much control I actually had in handling my problems. She made me realize that I was the one putting pressure on myself by trying to live up to my own unrealistic expectations.

Mrs. Cruz identified with my personal and academic struggles. She was a mentor, a role model, and a friend. She had always seen something in me that I often didn't see in myself. She not only helped me, but she empowered me as well.

That day truly shifted my perspective about my opportunities and how exciting it will be to see what the future holds.

I Didn't Give Up

Long before Monika Blaumueller became a TED speaker about big data analytics, she was a student at Michigan State University. Her college story touches on being shy, being resilient, and not being afraid to take risks:

Sophomore year at Michigan State, I took a Business German class and landed a paid internship at Bosch, the German multinational. My predecessor explained that this opportunity started when the head of technical training at Bosch invited the daughter of a friend in Michigan to intern in his department and live in his family's guest room.

My mistake was in assuming that Mr. Bohne would also invite me to live with his family. I was too shy to call or write to introduce myself. They had no idea that I was coming.

So I found myself in Stuttgart in the fall of 1988 with a job but no place to live. I was homeless, I didn't know anyone, and the dialect was hard to understand. I stayed in a youth hostel, which was tricky because I couldn't leave my suitcases there during the day. I would get up at 5 a.m. every weekday, move my luggage to a locker in the train station, and then take a series of trains and buses to make it to the office on time. After work, I'd go to the hostel, check if there was a vacancy, and schlep my suitcases uphill.

Work wasn't going well either. I was assigned to an isolated office where they didn't want a foreigner. I was relegated to mind-numbing tasks. I was broke. There was a problem with my visa. The office for work permits was discouraging. I remember sitting on a picturesque hillside vineyard at sunset, asking myself why I should stay.

One evening, I camped out in front of a dorm, where I found a sublet from someone who became, and remains, a good friend. Life at Bosch got better, too. The director of the division discovered where I was interning and then assigned me to interesting work in the big, central headquarters. I now had really cool colleagues, my commute was simple, and the dorm provided an immediate social life.

I was also finally invited to meet Mr. Bohne. We hit it off. He invited me home to dinner with his family. I moved into their guest room and we all became very close.

He asked me to work for him. I found myself running a month-long Christmas charity event sponsored by Bosch, Daimler-Benz, and Porsche. I worked with the governor and other local celebrities. I gave progress reports to a count, who was a Daimler-Benz executive. I got to act as a backup singer and dancer to a local Motown group. I also emceed some events that were broadcast on national radio.

It ended up being such a good experience that I spent the following year in Germany as an exchange student at a nearby university. That was 1989–1990. I spent New Year's Eve dancing on the Berlin Wall. I had the time of my life.

None of this would have happened if I hadn't taken a leap into a scary unknown, or stayed in Germany even when everything was going wrong.

At around the same time Monika was in Germany, Julia Karpeisky was making her way from Moscow to Kentucky. Here is her story, including how she ended up with a 2-year scholarship:

Not everyone gets to say that his or her picture was on the front page of the *Lexington Herald-Leader*. I do, and that's because, in the fall of 1990, I became the first Soviet graduate student at the University of Kentucky. Obviously, there is a story here, and every time I look back, I am amazed at how everything just aligned perfectly for me. I am grateful to all the people who helped me along the way.

I came to the United States a short 6 months earlier, alone, at the ripe age of 25, with $200, two suitcases, and a visitor's visa that did not allow me to work. I had a semester-long arrangement with a small college in Tennessee to teach a Russian conversation class in exchange for the airfare, a bed in the dorm, and a meal ticket.

After a couple of days on campus, I went to see Dean Harmon Dunathan at Rhodes College, the person who had brought me there. I handed him the return ticket, since I knew I was not going back. What I didn't know was how I was going to do it.

"You should talk to Dr. Michta," said Dean Dunathan. He is from Poland and he managed to stay in the United States. Dr. Michta taught a course about the future of communism.

Dr. Michta suggested that I apply to a graduate school and sent me to the library to pick a school.

I picked up the directory of graduate schools, a heavy tome with thin pages and tiny fonts, and got a huge knot in my stomach. What was I supposed to do with all these options? I headed back to Dr. Michta's office, but his door was now locked. Unsure what to do next, I stared at a colorful poster on the door from the Patterson School of Diplomacy and International Commerce at the University of Kentucky. Having studied only science and math in Russia, I didn't quite understand what that meant, but I liked the motto: "If we are not having fun, we are not doing it right." I filled out a card asking for more information and sent it in.

I discovered I was supposed to write a statement and submit three personal and professional references after only having been in the United States for less than 2 months. Didn't Dr. Michta say it was easy?

It must have been the novelty of having a Soviet applicant, but somehow I made it through the first cut and the Patterson School invited me for an interview. "I am sorry, I can't come," I said on the phone. "I don't have enough money to pay for the plane ticket or even a bus ticket from Memphis to Lexington."

I figured nothing else was going to happen with the Patterson School, so I proceeded with having my wisdom teeth removed. I was lying in bed, in pain, floating in and out of fevered sleep, when I heard the phone ring.

"It's for you," said Sarah, my roommate and a Russian major.

I shook my head.

"She is not here right now. Can I take a message?"

I dosed off to the murmur of Sarah talking on the phone.

"Julia!" she screamed. "Wake up! We are going shopping. You need a suit!"

"Sarah, I don't need a suit. I need to sleep. I am sick. Besides, I don't have the money, anyway."

"Julia, you are going to Lexington tomorrow. 7 a.m. flight. The school bought you a ticket! You are so lucky, I cannot believe it!"

Sarah's reaction made no sense to me, but that was true about a lot of things at that point. I thought that is how they normally do it in the United States: the school will buy you a ticket to come for an interview if you can't afford it yourself.

At the Blue Grass Airport in Lexington, I was greeted by Karin Stromqvist, a first-year Patterson School student from Sweden. She took me straight to campus, where I met a man who would became my teacher and my mentor, without whom my life in the United States would have never happened. But that day, Dr. Vince Davis, the Patterson School director, seemed scary and intimidating.

I learned that once a year, the school organizes a Model United Nations event for local high school students. They pick an area of the world to focus on and invite experts to talk about the region. It so happened that that year's region was Eastern Europe, and the event was actually that night. They wanted me to be part of the panel discussion.

25

I smiled politely and nodded, since the only thing I understood was Eastern Europe and discussion. I could totally do that, I thought—sit around and talk about Eastern Europe.

It was not until Karin took me to her house and introduced me to her roommates that I realized that panel discussion meant that I was going to be part of the panel, which involved sitting up on stage and talking into a microphone.

I felt my body shivering from the inside out. Who knew whether it was my fever or the overwhelming panic about having to go on stage and speak in front of hundreds of people in a foreign language after only having been in the country for such a short time?

"Forget it," I said, fighting back tears. "I am sick. I can't do it, I won't do it, I'll just take a nap here and go back to Memphis tomorrow."

And that's when I got yelled at like there was no tomorrow. "What? You are crazy! What do you mean you can't do it? This is a once in a lifetime opportunity! You can tell them the truth, you can tell them the truth about life in your country. This is your opportunity, your chance to stay in the United States. You have to do it!" All three of Karin's roommates were talking at the same time and interrupting each other.

In the midst of all this commotion, the doorbell rang. Someone sent me a bouquet of roses. An unsigned note said, "Good Luck!"

My stage fright was transformed into an adrenaline rush the minute I set foot on the stage. Once I was in front of the crowd of people, I felt excited, focused, and at my best.

Most of the questions were addressed to me, and I must have done a good job answering them. It so happened that some key people from a local Rotary Club were in the audience that day, and they were sufficiently impressed to provide me with a 2-year scholarship to attend the Patterson

School of Diplomacy and International Commerce. Dr. Davis arranged for the university to cover the rest.

That's how my picture made it to the front page of the *Lexington Herald-Leader*.

Katherine Vogel Anderson, a graduate of Florida State University and now a Clinical Assistant Professor at the University of Florida College of Pharmacy, reflects on how her struggles during college and graduate school have contributed to her pharmacy career:

I had to work two jobs during the summer and one job during the school year, not to mention taking really hard classes as a biochemistry major and then as a pharmacy student. I couldn't afford the airplane tickets to attend my father's retirement from the U.S. Army or my grandmother's funeral—and I couldn't have missed that much class and work anyway. At the end of the semester, when my loans started to run thin, I wondered if I would be able to pay all the bills (without asking my parents for help). I am really glad that I had to struggle. Learning to get through the struggle has been imperative to my success as a pharmacist.

Jennifer Laszlo Mizrahi, president of RespectAbility, shares how she overcame two big obstacles at Emory University:

College enabled me to reinvent myself. I was no longer the bullied idiot of my childhood. I learned to not have my head down in the dirt but, rather, to reach for the stars. In almost every class, I sat near the front of the room and asked questions.

Before college, all I could see was what I could not do because of my dyslexia. Pre-Emory, I was the kid who was bullied and taunted because I couldn't really read or write well, compared with my peers.

27

At Emory, I overcame the chronic insecurities that came from my learning disabilities and began to understand that I am what is now referred to as "twice exceptional"—which means that I have a disability and that I am also "gifted."

In college, I got a part-time job and used the money to hire other students to type my papers for me. I did the research and wrote the words, but in the pre–spell check era, I was incapable of getting through even a single sentence without a spelling mistake. After the paid typists cleaned up my spelling, my papers and other assignments reflected my thinking instead of my spelling. People saw what I could do. Indeed, I found that I really could do a lot of things very well.

I overcame another obstacle as well. In the first few days of my senior year at Emory, I was run over by a car. It was a very serious situation, with a lot of operations and pain. I needed to use a wheelchair. This occurred before the Americans with Disabilities Act had been passed and it was impossible for me to get to my classes. Back then, the buildings, curbs, and sidewalks were not accessible.

When I was physically hurt, people spoke loudly and slowly to me—as if I were hearing impaired or had an intelligence problem. I learned a lot about stigmas toward people with disabilities.

By the end of my senior year, I got better and no longer needed a wheelchair. I have overcome every aspect of dyslexia, except that I still can't do math and I still rely heavily on spell check.

For many years, I was not active in the disabilities movement, as I focused on politics, communications, faith-based work, and other initiatives. Today, I am proud to be one of many leaders in the disabilities movement.

Mark S. graduated from the University of Virginia's master's program in computer science after overcoming a difficult first semester:

After graduating from undergraduate school in the SUNY system with a Bachelor of Science in Computer Science/Mathematics, I wanted to further my education in computer science. I decided to look into graduate school. I wanted to go out of the New York area to broaden my personal experiences. I had researched the University of Virginia as a potential graduate school because of its beauty and its good computer science department. I had not been accepted to UVA as an undergraduate, but it was still a dream of mine to go there.

The private universities were very expensive, and I was not likely to get a lot of financial aid. As a state university, UVA had cheaper tuition even at the higher out-of-state rate. I applied and was accepted. I was offered a teaching assistantship, which enabled me to afford the tuition.

But there was one catch. I was accepted on probation and was required to maintain a 3.0 grade point average during my first semester.

The curriculum was very challenging. The computer science classes were highly theoretical and were at a totally different level than my undergraduate courses had been.

Sometimes, I really felt I was out of my league. So my first semester at UVA was not filled with confidence. My stress level was very high. Well, at the end of the semester, my GPA was 2.33—far below the required 3.0 GPA.

I got the call from the chairman of the computer science department that I knew was coming. I was being thrown out of the program. I pleaded with him to reconsider, but he said that the decision was final.

My morale was very low, and my dream was shattered. I initially didn't know what I would do next. I had made good friends at UVA and didn't want to go back to New York. I put so much work into getting there and into my courses, even though my grades didn't show it.

I just didn't want to give up. I figured that if I got an A in two more courses, it would bring my GPA up to 3.0. A long shot, to be sure, but it gave me a hopeful goal.

So I enrolled in a continuing education computer science course (in operating systems). I was on much firmer footing and did well. I got an A in the class.

Then I went to the computer science department chairman and pitched my idea about being readmitted to the department if I earned an A in another course. Normally, that kind of irregular idea would scare me off, but I felt the A in operating systems proved the potential that I had. He agreed to my proposal and put in writing that I needed to get at least an A- to be readmitted to the master's program.

I then enrolled in summer school, where I took a graduate-level course in probability and statistics. I also felt more at ease in that course and received an A. I was accepted back into the Computer Science program. My dream was revived.

Unfortunately, the stress did not end there. I still worried about doing well and was nervous about how some grades would turn out. After a lot of hard work, though, I graduated with a Master of Computer Science degree, and with no loss of time, finishing in the expected two years. My final GPA was 3.3, up almost a full point from my first semester.

This experience was a life lesson in perseverance. Sometimes I want to give up on difficult tasks or goals, but I learned I can succeed if they are important to me and reasonably in reach.

My University of Virginia diploma still hangs on my bedroom wall. I'm proud of it to this day.

The college-career connection is at the root of author Carol Christen's story about an elevator ride at UCLA that had a large impact on her career:

30

The threat of being a fifth-year senior in college has been around much longer than most people realize. While Neil Armstrong was keeping up his fitness routine prior to his giant leap for mankind, I was scuttling around UCLA frantically seeking to find open classes for summer term. Five classes in my major still remained. If I was unable to take those classes that summer, my college career would be extended into the next academic year. This was not acceptable. John Wooden, Pauley Pavilion, and the cultural banquet that was Los Angeles notwithstanding, I wanted out (although I must note that my then-classmate and future Kareem Abdul-Jabbar was a model of graciousness when I careened around a building and into his majestic person).

The day before the deadline to add summer classes, I was tapping my toes in an excruciatingly slow elevator in the social sciences building. I had just learned there was no room in a class I thought a decent substitute for my cancelled first choice. I had less than an hour to make it across campus to beg the enrollment office into letting me take the second substitution on my list, when my elevator mate halted the closing elevator door for one of his colleagues. The subsequent elevator conversation centered on the recent edict from the chancellor that full professors would need to take on teaching more undergraduate courses. Students were grumbling about not graduating in 4 years due to a lack of sufficient sections of lower and upper division classes required for graduation. Neither professor was happy about Chancellor Clark Kerr's solution that professors were to teach, not just research. As though I were invisible, both dapperly suited men vociferously objected to teaching non–graduate students, a time waster that added no value to their research. Teaching at this public university was beneath them.

From frustration, a vow was born. As I exited the elevator and began my cross-campus trek, I determined that someday, I would teach an undergraduate class in something totally practical. Eight years later, I got my chance. I was hired as an adjunct professor to teach career planning in the management department at Sonoma State University (and later went on to write *What Color Is Your Parachute for Teens*).

Solving Problems

Swarthmore College graduate Kiki Skagen Munshi attributes her ability to deal with the world's complexities to her liberal arts education:

Probably the most important thing I gained from my superb liberal arts education was how to deal with complexity. I learned first that there are few easy answers to anything. I then learned how to make decisions in spite of that, while remaining open to new information that might change what I already thought I knew.

The most direct link between college and my career in the Foreign Service was probably in Sierra Leone, West Africa, in 1993, after the Valentine Strasser coup. With a certain amount of pressure, the 25-year-old Strasser and others who had taken over the country decided to have "the people" vote on what form of government they wanted: presidential or parliamentary? Should there be proportional representation? How do you have majority rule but protect minorities (from, among other things, being killed)? This was quite a challenge in a country with high illiteracy, poor schools, almost nonexistent internal communications, and few such modern conveniences as government-supplied electricity.

I was head of the U.S. Information Service (USIS) in our Freetown Embassy. My all–Sierra Leonean staff and I decided that civic education materials were needed. We set to work. This was before the Internet and no one aside from my college political theory professor bothered to answer letters. So out came the old Sabine political theory text, which I had hauled around the world. You never know what books might be important.

What should a government do? What should a government not do? How do you structure things to get where you want to go? We came up with four sets of materials on basic questions, tested them on a group of high school teachers, and then set out up-country.

Let's be honest: We probably didn't make much difference, but there is more than one indelible memory. The most vivid one occurred at night under a tent by the light of the USIS generator (no electricity, so we brought our own). A market lady got up, nodded her head in greeting, and said—in essence—that there should be regular elections to throw out leaders when "they become thieves and steal our money."

Sierra Leone has a functioning democracy today, but between then and now, people had to live through the horrors of an extraordinarily brutal civil war. But at least some people understood that their opinions were important. And they mattered because they could vote.

Emily L., a 2008 graduate of Carnegie Mellon University, recounts her lessons from theater school:

What has stuck with me the most from my theater conservatory experience is the idea that "anything is possible as long as you have the money." This is a direct quote from one of our professors, who was describing how a technical director, the person in charge of actually building a set, should approach budgeting the often-preposterous ideas of the set designer. The idea is to never say "no" outright to creativity, that you are there to serve the expression of ideas, and that the need to keep those ideas within the realm of reality should be directed at editing the idea to make it more concise and clever.

I am struck regularly by the number of managers who seemed to have never learned this lesson. Instead, there is a lot of "No, we can't afford that" or "We don't do that" or "That's not industry standard" without any room for discussion. These managers believe they are doing their jobs and being helpful. However, a flat "no" to an idea teaches idea-havers to be more careful about what they express and hope to accomplish, and this can have a chilling effect that is far more damaging to innovation than occasionally overbudget or unsuccessful projects. The theater world is filled with overbudget and unsuccessful projects, but many of the projects that do manage to succeed would not have done so without the preceding years of their creators experiencing and learning from failure.

Another lesson from theater school is that everyone and everything is interesting if you know how to look at it. Figure drawing taught me that every body is beautiful. Spending hours painting faux-brick and marble taught me that every surface tells a story. We were taught that if you didn't like the play you were working on, the burden was on you to find something in it to keep you interested.

My favorite lessons, though, are from a professor who had a running joke about a class he would teach on all the weird bits of wisdom you need to learn to function in a theater environment. This included how to carry things backward down the stairs, how to charm a supplier on the phone into giving you a discount, and how to learn and move on from getting fired. My favorite, and the one that I repeat often, is how to assign blame when something goes wrong. To paraphrase him, "Listen, you're going to have these nights where rehearsal is over and it's been a disaster and it's like 2:00 in the morning and everyone is just going to be wallowing in figuring out who to blame. When that happens, the best thing to do is to say 'It's my fault' even if it's not your fault, because in those moments you just need to move on and get things done." While this is the last piece of advice I would give to someone being charged with a crime, it goes to the question at the heart of any legal argument, which is "What is relevant here?" Answering the question "Who is to blame?" often tells us nothing about how to move forward or what to do next, and even if it is relevant, it's not a conversation for 2 a.m. the night before previews.

Dr. Robert Wald, a physician and a member of the first graduating class at the Bronx High School of Science, attended Arizona State University, the University of California, Berkeley, and Washington University School of Medicine in St. Louis. He shares an amusing story from his medical school days:

There we were, volunteered captives of our Professor of Surgery, standing at the bed of Farmer Brown, his patient about whom we were to learn something very significant.

Four intimidated medical students with the Professor, almost Herr Professor, giving us our chance to learn.

With his hand on crutches resting on the radiator next to the bed, the Professor allowed each of us to ask the patient three questions to determine the cause and effect of his hospital stay.

With his stentorian voice, the Professor revealed that this patient had received what was then a new surgery, replacing his critically impaired femoral arteries. Hand still on the crutches, our Leader declared, "Farmer Brown came to the hospital on these stalks but returns to his fields on restored legs."

Tall as he was and short as I am, I sidled closer, raising my eyes to meet his downward glaze, my hand upon his, still atop the crutches and offered, "Sir, may I take the crutches down to the chapel?"

My classmates' gasps were met by our Leader's smile.

Roland Machold served as State Treasurer of New Jersey from 1999 until 2001. He fondly remembers one particular moment from his undergraduate days at Yale:

My junior year, I took a Classical Studies course with a Swiss professor, and I completely forgot about a special assignment for our final exam. I called and made the usual excuses—sickness, urgent family business, etc., all intended to buttress my plea for a postponement, but my professor wasn't buying any of it. I had to take the test right now, in his office. I knew I was doomed.

I entered his office as a condemned man. However, he first wanted to take the edge off of his rough manner, so he asked me one perfunctory personal question. "Where are you going this summer?" I said that my family was going to a little town in the Swiss Alps called Champex, so that I could continue my climbing interests. He looked up, astonished. That was his hometown! Oh, what a good idea, and I must do this and I must do that, and I must go to this restaurant, and I must hire that guide. After a while, it occurred to him that I had to take a test. He looked at his watch, and after a pause, asked what grade I had received on my midterm exam, and I said an 85. "Good," he said, "then that is the grade for your final exam." Since then, I have always loved the study of classics.

Edie Maddy-Weitzman attended Brandeis University in the early 1970s. Here are her thoughts about being reduced to a category—and what she did about it:

At Brandeis, I was drawn to the field of sociology because of the influences of two wonderful professors—Charles Derber and the late Morrie Schwartz (of *Tuesdays with Morrie*). At their recommendation, I took a class at a leadership training center in neighboring Cambridge.

This was a time when encounter group–style courses were very popular as a therapeutic method, and the center's purpose was to train people to facilitate group encounters. The participants ranged in ages from college age to late adulthood. Each week, a different student prepared group exercises that would facilitate discussion. I was drawn to a young woman of my age named Maureen and, in the early stages of the class, we often spent breaks together. I began to consider her a friend. One day I mentioned to her that I had recently spent my junior year abroad in Israel at the Hebrew University of Jerusalem.

During the next meeting, it was Maureen's turn to lead the group and she did so by creating a group sculpture, placing the members with whom she felt closest nearest to her. To my surprise, she placed me at the furthest edge of the group. When I later asked her why she had distanced me so, she replied that she could never be close to a Jew (she had only realized that I was Jewish when I mentioned to her that I had spent the year in Israel).

I was stunned and shocked. As I write this now, I still vividly recall the feelings of helplessness and powerlessness that came from being reduced to a category. I quickly understood that there was nothing I could say or do that could penetrate her wall of hostility.

Following the group session, which had reduced me to tears, I had several conversations with Professor Derber and Professor Schwartz about what had transpired. We spoke about the harmful effects of stereotyping, prejudice, and discrimination. As a result of their words, I did not allow myself to wallow in pity about what had taken place.

Years later, living in Israel, I was directly exposed to the conflict between Israelis and Palestinians and the negative stereotypes each side held toward the other. To be sure, these were primarily rooted in the long-running, seemingly intractable conflict between them, but also from the lack of direct contact between individuals in their respective communities.

To my good fortune, I was exposed to Seeds of Peace, an organization that worked with Palestinian and Israeli teenagers, with the goal of training some of the future leaders of the Middle East. Getting the participants to see beyond the labels of "Israeli" or "Palestinian" and viewing each other as human beings, all of whom deserved to live honorably in a more just world, is central to its mission. The encounters between them were often highly charged, and participants also faced hostility within their own communities for the very notion of meeting with "the enemy."

I was so impressed with the courage of these teenagers in their willingness, and even eagerness, to get to know members of the other side that I volunteered to be a college counselor for the Palestinian and Israeli teens who wanted to apply to American universities. I am grateful to my two professors from long ago, for I now realize that their words later inspired me to help youth living in a conflict zone to have a chance for a better life. I share the Seeds of Peace program's hope that these adolescents, through their experiences and education, will one day contribute to the resolution of this conflict.

Mistakes Revisited

Robert Tomkin, a graduate of the University of New Hampshire, and now a writer at Congressional Quarterly, reflects on his college years and on how he wishes he had taken a particular poetry class:

I wish I had taken better advantage of everything college had to offer, including the academic, social, and even the spiritual. College can be a once-in-a-lifetime experience. Never again will you have so little responsibility and so much freedom. Take it all in. Don't spend all of your time on one thing, whether it is partying, traveling, or even studying. I wish I had studied more, but an all-encompassing study regime should not be at the expense of actual learning. They are not always the same. See Steve Jobs.

Don't confine yourself to preconceived notions, whether they are academic, intellectual, or social. Try not to just follow the group. Expose yourself to different ideas, different people, and different experiences. Join groups that you will never join again. Listen to speakers you may never listen to again. Befriend people you might never befriend again. And certainly take classes you might never take again.

During my last semester at UNH, I was part of a student/faculty group tasked with bringing prominent speakers to campus. One of the faculty representatives taught a course on poetry. I had no interest in taking such a class. However, after spending time with him, I came to understand that it was the teacher, not the subject area, that often matters most. I regret not taking his class.

In the end, remember to explore and question everything. Learn to question from positions based on fact, not just opinion. Don't be afraid to fail. Most explorers fail more often than they succeed. But those who have the audacity to challenge their own comfort zones ultimately attain heights they never imagined they could attain.

Gordon Rooney, development manager for the City of Charleston Office of Cultural Affairs and a 2010 University of Texas graduate, was active politically in Austin but wishes he had gotten more involved on campus:

I chose to attend the University of Texas at Austin for a number of reasons. One of them was because of the many internship opportunities in state government in Austin. Not only did I intern at the state capitol, but I also worked on multiple political campaigns. When I wasn't in class, these off-campus adventures were where I focused my time and energy.

UT has the Texas Union, a large student center with many student organizations. On reflection, my experience as a student might have been enhanced had I been more involved with these groups and other campus activities.

Through the Texas Union, I went to a student leadership camp where I met many wonderful people. I attended some meetings for the Distinguished Speakers Committee and the Recreation Committee, but I didn't run for office or attend those meetings regularly. I think my mind was elsewhere, like on those off-campus opportunities I could be taking advantage of, which I did. Perhaps I got bored and just didn't give some of the student groups a chance to make an impact on my college experience.

I was involved with a student-run political group and I attended book discussions through UT Austin's Thomas Jefferson Center for the Study of Core Texts and Ideas. These discussions were held at the Texas Union but not part of the Texas Union's committees. I also spent nearly 5 months in D.C. through the Archer Fellowship Program. We lived on Capitol Hill, worked full time (mostly through internships), and studied advocacy, public policy, and politics in the evenings and on the weekends. I still keep in touch with many of the Fall 2008 Archer Fellows.

One of the most important reasons to get involved in your campus community is that you'll make new friends. I met one of my best friends in class; we just started talking one day after class and it grew from there. I met another good friend through Air Force ROTC. With the exception of my two brothers, all of the groomsmen in my wedding were friends I met in college.

In hindsight, I probably would have made even more friends at UT if I had been more active on campus. Making new friends and developing meaningful friendships will make your overall campus experience better—and joining one or more student organizations is a direct and easy way to do that.

Bill Caldwell, a 1997 landscape architecture graduate of the University of Georgia, regrets not attending his graduation ceremonies:

The weather that weekend was awful and both my wife and I were focused on starting our upcoming jobs and getting on with the next phase of our lives. I look back now and realize that graduation would have been an excellent time to say goodbye to some of the friends I had made at UGA. I made a mistake not to participate.

Trooper Sanders, a graduate of the University of Michigan and the London School of Economics, and later a Domestic Policy Advisor to President Bill Clinton, reflects on his education:

My biggest education regret was not pursuing an undergraduate degree at a foreign university. The United States is blessed to have some of the world's best colleges and universities. But the world also offers an extraordinary range of top schools, in interesting places, that provide unique experiences both in life and education. A simple

Internet search puts finding these schools at your fingertips, and many programs that offer an awesome experience cost the same if not less than having a ho-hum experience at home.

Professional tour guide Pete McCall had a two-part college career, which was separated by 2 years in the Navy Reserve. He explains:

My two-part college career was checkered. Upon graduation from a Presbyterian military prep school, McCallie School in Chattanooga, I matriculated at the University of Tennessee, Knoxville. As a rebellious, mischievous prankster, I was placed on social probation for telling jokes on a tape in French class. The next year, I was caught on the 8th floor of the freshman girls' dorm (then off-limits to males). I was in hot water. After suspension from college, my father decided I should serve in the military to "get my act together." In hopes of shaping up, I shipped out and spent two years of active duty in the Navy Reserve as a hospital corpsman in Hawaii.

While stationed with sailors who lacked the opportunity for advanced education, I came to realize the importance of earning a college degree. I was ready then to seriously continue my college career in my hometown of Chattanooga. I buckled down, studied hard, performed in several plays, and earned my bachelor's degree in history. One reason why I majored in history was because, as a teenager, I was very interested in the Civil War. Yes, I still partied and enjoyed myself at the University of Tennessee at Chattanooga, but I managed to keep out of trouble. I also developed a continuing love of history, literature, drama, and art.

Learning to Adapt

Jonathan Blyth, Commander in the United States Navy Reserve, reflects on his time at Franklin & Marshall College and the importance of friendship:

Franklin & Marshall College was tough. The classes were challenging but excellent. The professors were extraordinary, but they would have been more willing to give away their first-born children then give away As. However, I got through the 4 years. I will always treasure my amazing undergraduate education.

In the classroom, I learned how to think, how to solve a problem, how to research an issue, and how to defend a theory. I believe I also learned a great deal outside the classroom.

Growing up in New York City, I wanted to have a true college experience with a campus. I wanted to live in a dorm, experience campus social life, and enjoy an experience in which everything was focused on the 4 years of college. Franklin & Marshall, located in the farm country of Lancaster, Pennsylvania, fit the bill perfectly.

I also wanted that fraternity experience. Even more, I wanted to become president of the fraternity. The Pennsylvania Eta Chapter of Phi Kappa Psi was a small fraternity. With so few brothers, I knew I would be a big fish in a small pond. I knew if I worked hard, I could become the president. That is how I had achieved all my leadership positions in high school.

Fourteen members joined the fraternity in the next pledge class after mine, which doubled the size of the brotherhood. Recruiting all these new members was a fellow classmate, William J. Hughes, Jr. Bill was the son of a Congressman from the state of New Jersey. He grew up in the world of politics and was a born leader and politician. His power of persuasion had led to the recruitment of the large pledge class, and he was my strongest rival.

The chapter continued to grow during my sophomore and junior years. Bill and I brought in new brothers. When a pledge who had been brought in by someone other than Bill or me became a brother, it became clear that his allegiance needed to be pledged to one side or another: Bill's brothers on one side and my brothers on the other side. Both Bill and I were working toward the goal of becoming president of the chapter. At that point, we were not fraternity brothers. We were, in a sense, direct competitors.

I can remember vividly when it was announced that William J. Hughes, Jr. was elected president of the fraternity. I was devastated, but I decided to serve as his vice president.

Over the next six months, I worked with Bill to execute his agenda. He had some big ideas and got some great things accomplished. Bill worked with me, and I with him, because we really needed each other. What he understood better than I did at the time was that we each really envied one another. We were both jealous of the other because each of us lacked some of the leadership skills the other had.

At a brothers meeting several months into his term, Bill announced that he would not run for reelection. The path to achieve my goal was finally clear, and I was elected president, and then reelected for a second term.

During those years, I learned some important lessons. When I lost to Bill, I learned that it is essential to put aside your own personal interests for the greater good. I also learned to accept defeat, to be gracious, and to push forward.

I also learned to listen to the concerns of my fellow fraternity brothers. I learned that leadership is about establishing goals and motivating individuals to achieve those goals. You really need to work very hard and to anticipate future actions in order to prepare how to react.

I took my college experiences and went to Washington, D.C. to serve as Chief of Staff to three Members of the House of Representatives and was a political appointee in the Bush Administration. Presently, I serve as a Commander in the United States Navy Reserve.

Bill went home to New Jersey, earned a master's degree from the Eagleton Institute of Politics at Rutgers University, then law degrees from Rutgers and Georgetown, and became a prominent attorney.

Most importantly, Bill and I have remained good friends, and we admit to this day that both our rivalry and our friendship have made us better people.

2008 Yale graduate Edward Dunar shares a story about a puppet named Uncle Fred that still remains a part of Edward's life:

I found a best friend and a valued mentor because of a puppet named Uncle Fred. A bald eagle with strong opinions, he sits on my desk to this day.

Uncle Fred's career started during my freshman year of college. I remember being exhilarated during my first week of class as I gathered my books—Plato, Homer, and Herodotus. At my very first seminar meeting, I sat down at a dark wood table in a room covered with bookshelves and portraits of distinguished scholars. This is what college is all about, I thought.

Class began. "I read this back in high school," one of my classmates remarked. "It gets better with every reading! This time around, it reminded me of something that Derrida wrote…"

And I had no idea what to say.

In retrospect, I realize that my classmates felt just as out of place as I did. But I didn't know that at the time. They seemed so confident (even joyous) during our discussions, and I always felt ten steps behind.

One late night at the end of the semester, I finally finished my readings for the week. As I prepared for the 3 hours of sleep ahead of me, I looked in the mirror and paused. I had always considered myself an optimistic person, but in my face, I saw the accumulated long nights and stresses of a semester. *This isn't who I am,* I thought. (I once saw a Red Bull poster that read, "Nobody wishes they would have slept more during college." Maybe I'm the first.)

It was time for drastic measures. But what? My eyes rested on Uncle Fred, the eagle puppet, who sat on my desk.

The next day, I raised my hand at the end of class and said, "For anyone who's interested... I'll be doing a puppet show after class next week." Silence. The professor raised his eyebrows. "All right, then."

My classmates laughed and clapped at an adventure starring Uncle Fred and a stuffed Winnie the Pooh from my childhood. The duo stormed Troy. They sang the lyric poetry of Petrarch to a tune of a popular song from that year. They descended through the layers of Dante's Inferno.

Years later, I ran across the script that I used for the show. Most of the jokes didn't make much sense. My classmates seemed to like the show, though. Even the professor, who had lingered by the door after class before deciding to stay, cracked a smile. For the first time, I felt as though I didn't have anything to prove to my classmates. There I was—a mediocre puppeteer and comedian—putting on the equivalent of an 8-year-old's garage puppet show. But it was the offbeat moment we all needed. My clumsy rebellion against the pressures and expectations of our first semester gave us all permission to be childish for a while.

I performed many puppet shows that year.

Brian was a guy from my residential hall who I hung out with from time to time. We weren't close friends at first. After realizing early on that we both did laundry on Friday nights (neither of us enjoyed the party scene), we had watched a James Bond movie or two together.

After one of my puppet shows, Brian approached with a wry grin. "You're a natural," he said. "While watching your show, I had a vision about you and me. In business together."

My first reaction was to laugh. My show certainly didn't merit a business offer. As we sat down at lunch in the dining hall, we talked about doing a comedy show on the campus cable network. We dreamed of doing a full-length movie after the first season. We could even make T-shirts! I found myself laughing harder than I had all semester.

On that day, we became lifelong friends.

I didn't end up going into either comedy or puppetry. In fact, when people remark, "I hear you're a puppet guy," I vehemently deny it. Real puppeteers are artists; I'm an occasional dabbler. But the puppets somehow find their way into whatever I'm doing. They helped my first grade students learn phonics. They added some levity to team meetings when I worked at a software company. Uncle Fred, in particular, has a way of making return appearances.

While attending an academic conference a few years ago, I grabbed lunch with one of my favorite professors from my undergrad years. We talked about memories, projects, and family. Before we went our separate ways, she touched my arm. "Do you know when I realized that I'd enjoy working with you? When you asked if you could do that puppet show." She smiled. "I had no idea how to respond! I wasn't going to say no in front of the whole class. But afterward, it reminded me of why I enjoy teaching."

Uncle Fred still sits at the top of my desk. Whenever I feel overwhelmed or discouraged, he reminds me that my life is more than whatever I happen to be worrying about. And he helps me realize that when I look back on my life, years from now, I won't remember the projects and accomplishments as much as the people.

Biologist Liz Droge-Young, a 2005 graduate of Colorado State University, recounts a funny story that relates to her biology and performing arts double major:

I had just inadvertently ripped the tail off the little rodent I was stuffing for my final project in Mammology. In this lab course, I was introduced to an interesting group of scientists, who, like plenty of other biologists I met, loved animals, but with one important difference: Mammologists also loved stuffing them.

I was in the middle of extracting the tail vertebrae from a tiny vole, which is like a rounder version of a mouse, when the accident happened. The thing was, I had been given this particular vole from a collection of rodents trapped as part of a research project, but supplies had run out. If I wanted a vole with an attached tail, I would either need to go find myself another live one or draw on the sewing skills from my second major.

In addition to my biology major, which had gotten me into the amateur taxidermy business for the semester, I also completed a second major in theatre, where I focused on costume design. Running with theatre and biology crowds was sometimes like living in two separate worlds. On the plus side, the biologists were wowed with my artistic abilities, although my aptitude was firmly in the average camp from a costume design perspective. Meanwhile, theatre kids were impressed that I had passed organic chemistry. But most often, I was met by surprise or confusion that I was double majoring in two seemingly disparate subjects. The truth is that both majors required an attention to detail and creative thinking, just applied to different challenges.

Back to my tailless vole. I knew there was no way that I would go out vole-hunting myself to collect another specimen; it was time for some sewing magic. I whipped out some needle and thread, and with a few quick stitches and

48

some sturdy knots, my vole had all its appendages secured once again. My lab mates congratulated me for my stitching skills.

When I shared my success with fellow costume shop workers, they were adequately grossed out. Most importantly, the professor who graded our taxidermied critters was none the wiser about my tail mishap.

And people say that biology and theatre aren't related.

Attorney Terence Fernando's story involves the Sri Lanka Bar Association, his student orientation at Penn Law School, a 2 a.m. economics discussion, and a 4 a.m. breakfast that eventually led to a conversation with a Nobel Prize winner. Terence's experiences demonstrate how interactions on and around campus can have an impact on one's future. We also see university life from the perspective of an international student who took full advantage of the multidisciplinary opportunities in front of him:

After a demanding academic trek through pre-university qualifying examinations, a Bachelor of Laws, and bar exams for admission as an Attorney-at-Law in Sri Lanka, I embarked on a lifelong wish to study at an overseas university. My choice was a Master of Laws program at the University of Pennsylvania Law School.

The first day at Penn was memorable for its orientation meetings, along with the wine and cheese parties, none of which I had been accustomed to at the state-run University of Sri Lanka. There, instead, thousands gathered on the opening day in a chaotic atmosphere to find their way through a bureaucratic maze.

Judge Arlin Adams of the U.S. Court of Appeals, 3rd Circuit, whom I was seeing for the first time, so I thought, but looked remotely familiar, gave an inspiring speech about the efficacy of the legal profession for its abilities to champion any cause. Of course, then I remembered where I had seen him before.

I went down to the podium and introduced myself. I said: "Judge Adams, I was in the audience when you addressed the Sri Lanka Bar Association in Colombo a few years ago!" He was ecstatic, because he least expected to meet at Penn Law School an attorney from Sri Lanka who also was in the audience when he was a guest speaker at its bar association a few years earlier. He was so excited that he went back to the microphone to introduce me as an attorney from Sri Lanka. So I started law school in the United States with 15 seconds of celebrity status!

Once classes began, my fellow students and I spent a great deal of time at the law school library that was open 24 hours a day. After studying, we would often walk to our respective apartments through Locust Walk, which cuts through the main campus, passing the famous Wharton School, where the offices and study rooms were always lit at any time of the day.

One night, when we were walking home at around 2 a.m., my friend and fellow LL.M. student spotted our mutual friend, Bob Mooradian, a Ph.D. economics student and adjunct professor, working in his office. My friend suggested we stop by to have a chat with Bob.

Even at 2 a.m., Bob was happy to see us. He studiously greeted us with an economics issue regarding the time value of money and zero coupon bonds. What originally was intended as just a chat turned into a lengthy discussion until 4 a.m. Bob suggested we have some breakfast. The obvious choice was a place a few blocks away called Troy's that served a princely four-egg omelet with toast and unlimited coffee for the price of $2.50, perfectly fitting our limited student budgets.

The "Penn effect" continued long thereafter: When I was interviewed for my second job at a prominent Philadelphia law firm, I was interviewed initially by a partner who had graduated from Penn Law School; had a follow-up interview with a senior partner, also a Penn Law graduate; and then had a final formal interview with the managing partner, also a Penn Law graduate.

Some time into the job, a partner with whom I was working on a case that opposed a U.S. computer giant called me to his office and asked that I line up an expert economist for future consultations regarding the case. My obvious choice was none other than Bob, the time-value-of-money and zero-coupon-bond guy who gave us a mini-class on the subject at 2 in the morning and who was by this time a professor of finance at the University of Florida.

Bob was thrilled to hear from me and, after a brief chat about our time at Penn, I mentioned to him the purpose of my call. He thanked me for having considered using him as an expert and for keeping the Penn spirit.

After a discussion about the case, I was flabbergasted when he said frankly that he was not good enough for this specific case. "[This Corporation] will retain one of the most prominent economists in the United States because money is not an issue for them. You must line up an economist who will have similar name recognition as theirs." Thereafter, Bob gave me three names and suggested that I contact them.

When I phoned the first, a professor from Cornell University, he didn't sound very enthusiastic about our case and took my phone number to call back, but he never did.

The second, a very conservative-sounding MIT professor, gave me a moment to argue my side of the case before launching into a 5-minute lecture, in effect saying that the corporation was right in what it did. He then practically hung up the phone on me.

The third, Professor Robert Merton from Harvard, listened politely to what the case was about after I introduced myself. We informally chatted about the case for about 10 minutes when he said: "I am a little busy this week because I am preparing to go overseas, but I will put you on to my secretary to make an appointment so that we can continue the conversation after my return." I thanked him for his time and wished him good luck on his trip.

While his secretary was checking his diary, I tried to make some small talk and asked whether Professor Merton was going on a vacation.

She said, "He was awarded the Nobel Prize in Economics this year [1997] and will be going to Sweden to accept it."

I literally fell off my chair. Looking back, I wonder whether his chat with me was serious or he was just being polite to a lesser mortal of life! Be that as it may, Penn came full circle to put me in contact with a Nobel Prize winner.

Marc Landis, a graduate of Princeton University and former chair of the Manhattan Democratic County Committee, shares a timeline from the end of his senior year:

Wednesday, April 18, 1984. Princeton requires every senior to write a senior thesis of scholarly merit (or equivalent project), under the guidance of a faculty member. I have printed out (from the University's old mainframe computer) the final version of my thesis, "Chicago: Old Machine or New Alliance?"—a study of Chicago politics following the historic election of its first African-American mayor, Harold Washington. I walk down the block from campus to deliver the thesis to the local bindery, knowing that I'll have submitted the finished effort on time. Just a few weeks left of classes, then graduation, my summer job, then off to law school.

Thursday, April 26, 1984. My advisor reminds me that the Department of Politics has one more requirement that must be satisfied before graduation: an essay-based comprehensive examination focused on a particular area of politics (American, international, comparative, or theoretical). I am preparing to find and review 4 years' worth of class notes to prepare for "comps" when my friend

Ira, also a politics major, comes to me with a proposal. Chris, another friend of ours, had reviewed the department requirements, and discovered that we had the right to request oral comprehensive exams instead of written. Chris, along with another classmate also named Chris, suggested that we take the concept a step further, and set up a Parliamentary-style debate in lieu of traditional oral examinations. This would allow us to do less work in preparation, since the presentation time would be shared by four of us. We were quite pleased with ourselves, and hoped the plan would work—but first, we take a few days off so we can enjoy "house parties" weekend at the clubs on Prospect Street.

Monday, May 7, 1984. The first step, of course, is getting the Department of Politics to approve our approach. Oral examinations traditionally are administered by a panel of three professors. But two would suffice. We convince a slightly skeptical former departmental chair, Professor Stanley Kelley, to serve as a judge. Tom Rochon, a young assistant professor who had arrived at Princeton with us in 1980, is happy to serve as the other judge. Our judges warn us that we need to be prepared to answer questions relating to our departmental studies in addition to our debate topic. We need a general debate topic that would allow us to show off the breadth and depth of our politics scholarship, and select: "Resolved, Congress should defer to the President in foreign policy matters." Chris and Chris, the two conservative Republicans, would take the affirmative; Ira and I, liberal Democrats, would challenge and rebut their Reagan-era positions. We prepare a formal program and a listing of our respective coursework.

Tuesday, May 15, 1984. Following a full weekend of last-minute debate prep and a survey of our notes from department classes (with extra focus on classes that had been taught by our judges), we are ready for the big day. We set up shop in one of the smaller classrooms in Corwin Hall (named for Department of Politics founder and constitutional scholar Edward Samuel Corwin), and kick off our debate. Our opponents present strict-constructionist opening arguments; Ira and I respond, challenging the premise of the "imperial Presidency" and emphasizing the critical role of Congress as a counterweight. Our judges pepper us with questions on our debate topic and test our knowledge of politics scholarship generally. As I recall, among the four of us we received two As, an A-, and a B+—a nice coda to the year.

Darshan Somashekar is a 2005 public policy graduate of Brown University. He shares how burritos in college influenced his post-college path:

There I stood, a freshman, hungry, and right in front of Bagel Gourmet. I had heard about this place. I heard about how the bagels had the right surface crunch and chewy, doughy middles. I knew about the secret Mexican food menu, the one that wasn't posted for the public to see. Once you ordered from the secret menu, it became impossible to turn back.

That's where I discovered the breakfast burrito with bacon. In the turbulent world of a college freshman, that burrito was the rock I could cling to—a soft tortilla, with just the right combo of protein, cheese, and pico de gallo (all of the important food groups, I might add).

I was enrolled in classes as well. The first major in which I took an interest was computer science. I had done some programming and made a few websites in high school and I thought this could be the way to go. But the long hours at the computer lab ended up being a quick deterrent. Through the haze of a late afternoon burrito, I realized that my love for computer science was on the wane and that my interest in public policy and political science was on the rise. I focused on statistics and the political process.

However, I realized that while I didn't want to major in computer science, I still wanted to create websites and be an entrepreneur. Unfortunately, Brown didn't have an undergraduate business school. So, even as I worked through my public policy major, I didn't know what to do next.

By this time, I was a listless senior unsure about my next step. As always, I went to my spiritual home. Halfway into a burrito, a friend of mine walked by and saw me. This friend had a far clearer grasp of her direction in life. She asked me what I was going to do after graduation. After seeing my lackadaisical attitude, she upbraided me and pushed me to go to an info session at a firm where she interned the summer before.

Having nothing better to do, I decided to go. It was fortuitous. The info session, by Bain and Company, opened me up to the possibilities of business, problem solving, and working with other ambitious people that both melded with my entrepreneurial leanings and gave me a challenge. I decided to apply, got in, met amazing coworkers, spent two years there, and then started two companies. The lesson learned? Always appreciate a good burrito—it can change your life.

Tom Sansone, a Connecticut attorney who serves as president of a nonprofit that provides technical and financial assistance to a school in rural western Kenya, traces his community service involvement to his student days at Boston University:

I grew up in a small town in western Connecticut, attending the local Catholic grammar school and the regional Catholic high school. I led a very sheltered existence, where the vast bulk of people with whom I interacted were white, middle-class Roman Catholics of Italian, Irish, or Polish extraction. When I arrived on the campus of Boston University to begin my freshman year, I experienced absolute culture shock, simultaneously feeling

55

both excited and terrified. I was immediately struck by the size and diversity of the student body, which at that time boasted a population of nearly 25,000, including graduate students. My own residence hall, the largest on campus, housed about 1,700 students, more than three times the size of my entire high school.

It would have been very easy to have gotten lost in the sea of anonymity of such an environment. Through a stroke of good fortune, I ended up on a "quiet floor" in this massive residence hall, where each student had agreed to maintain an atmosphere conducive to good study habits. Don't misunderstand me—this was no monastery. The 40 or so residents of this floor still played their music loud, roughhoused in the corridors, and made plenty of noise. But a group of upperclassmen more than managed to keep the freshmen in line, setting a good example of how to work hard in addition to playing hard.

Four of these upperclassmen "adopted" me almost as soon as I arrived on campus. Jim was a fellow Connecticut resident, who grew up in nearby Bridgeport. Dave was a wisecracking Falstaff-like figure from Cranston, Rhode Island. Bob was a preppy kid from the suburbs of Providence. And Alex was a big, lovable bear from Manchester, about an hour north of Boston.

You couldn't have found four more different people. Yet we got along famously, and acceptance by these four popular upperclassmen greased the skids of my transition to college life. It was Jim who persuaded me to run for the student government position as the representative of our floor. With all four of them supporting me, my victory was assured. Over the course of that year, the five of us revamped the residence hall's weekly newspaper, took charge of the dorm's Wooden Nickel Pub, and put together a winning ticket when I ran for president of the student government in the spring (with Bob as my treasurer).

Being with those four guys my freshman year was pivotal for me. They were great friends but also great role models. They spent plenty of time at their studies, but they also knew how to have fun when the books were put away. Most importantly, they showed me how it was cool to be involved in service to the community through our dorm activities. That experience and that understanding helped set in motion the course that I would follow for the rest of my college career. My 4 years were filled with meetings, planning sessions, fundraisers, lots of studying, and lots of fun.

Years later, when I graduated from law school, I decided to take a break from all those commitments. Yet, within a few months, I found that I felt empty and bored. Community service had become part of me, and I could no sooner give it up than I could give up working at my profession. And now, many years after graduating from college, I find that I'm still as delightfully busy and engaged as I was during my years as an undergraduate at BU. I'll be forever grateful to the four upperclassmen who, for no apparent reason, thought it was important to take me under their collective wings and act as mentors for me.

Former United States Ambassador to Azerbaijan Richard Kauzlarich shares what he learned about responsibility and relating to adults when he was a student at Black Hawk College:

My experience at Black Hawk, a junior college in Moline, Illinois, taught me more about how to deal with real-life challenges than any other part of my college experience did. It taught me to value the importance of hard work and responsibility. I worked during the day at a bank in Moline and went to classes in the evening. I knew that my folks did not have the money to pay for my college education. Neither of my parents went to college. In fact, only my mother graduated from high school. All they knew was that learning was important for success in life. That encouragement was all I needed.

The other important lesson I learned was how to relate to adults outside my family. Most of my fellow students were much older than I was. I learned from them that education was really a lifelong process.

Jim Gelb, California State University's Assistant Vice Chancellor for Federal Relations, shares how his Pennsylvania to Wyoming transition helped him when he enrolled as an undergraduate at Harvard:

On a spring morning toward the end of my sophomore year of high school in Scranton, Pennsylvania, my parents called a family meeting to announce—quite unexpectedly— that we were moving. And not across town, or downstate, but to Laramie, Wyoming, a place I had never heard of, let alone visited. It was a pretty daunting change at what seemed a less than optimal time, as I had a good life and had been doing well in school in the only hometown I had ever known. My classmates, teachers, and community knew me, and I had a good feel for what was expected of me. Now I would be in a place where none of that held true. But it was exciting too—a new, exotic landscape to explore and customs to learn. I also had the extreme good fortune of making some new friends before my junior year officially started who eased my transition through such shared interests as playing in the marching band and enjoying pick-up basketball.

Two years later, when I again moved across the country to begin my freshman year at Harvard, I noticed that many of my classmates, all highly successful high school students, struggled at first to adapt to their new surroundings. Most eventually did, but many found their freshman year to be less enjoyable than I did. I realized that my move at age 16 had been a blessing in disguise, as it helped me understand that I could leave a comfortable place for a new environment where no one knew anything about me, and still have fun and thrive. Of course, you don't need to change time zones to achieve this; hopefully, all of us can locate confidence in a transition we survived before going to college and draw on that experience to help us relax and enjoy the new opportunities and challenges that await.

Anne Arnold was an English major at the University of Michigan and is now director of educational programs at the American Congress of Obstetricians and Gynecologists. She shares how she learned to expand her concept of village:

I come from a small village in the Midwest. And when I write "village," I mean a very small Irish–Polish Catholic village of about 50 families in the midst of thousands of acres of cornfields and cow pastures. Even the length of our driveway, at about 100 yards, is a journey by L.A. standards.

The population of my village is quite homogeneous. We share a Northern European background, were raised Catholic, and came from fiscally conservative farming or working-class families. In primary school, most kids' hair was blond or red. In high school, there was one person of color in my graduating class of 200 students. Thinking back, he was actually the only kid from a minority group in the entire school.

One day in late August, I left the village. My mom and dad drove me 2 hours across the state to leave me there, on campus. Once we arrived, I remember seeing a few things for the first time in my life that I will never forget.

As my parents helped me move my things into the dorm, I happened to see a group of Jewish boys heading out the door, each one wearing a yarmulke. Upstairs in my hall, I noticed the women in one family dressed in traditional saris. They were chanting a traditional puja to bless the daughter's room before they left. Then I heard another family speaking Vietnamese with their son as they helped him get his suitcase up the stairs. That boy later became one of my closest friends, and we're still friends 20 years later. My roommate pointed out at some point that I contributed to the mix as the only redhead in our wing.

It was at college that I met friends and professors with whom I shared ideas. As a result, my views were broadened and my perspectives changed about life, love, politics, war, poverty, and everything else. I learned that the most open minded of people are those who fully listen to others explain their ideas, even when they completely disagree.

Today, I am grateful for everything I learned through my friends, who opened my eyes, heightened my curiosity, and challenged my ideas. In many ways those ideas, stemming from diverse perspectives, molded who I have become. In fact, as a direct result of my college experience, I lived and studied abroad, have taught in many countries, including India, Sweden, and Latvia, and am now able to speak three languages well.

Clearly, much of what I learned at college happened outside of the classroom and made me a better person. I haven't forgotten my roots, though, and am happy to return a few times a year to my small village to visit family, friends, open pastures, and the cows.

University of Miami graduate Rebecca Chura writes about her grandmother, Adelaide Miller, who was an administrator at the University of Miami. Rebecca's story shows the impact of her grandmother both on and off the Miami campus, which to this day supports a well-known football program:

In the '70s, just three blocks east of the coveted Coral Gables, there lived a short, sweet woman in a quaint yellow house who spent her days working for the Dean of Women at the University of Miami. She spent her nights caring for her two small grandchildren. This woman worked tirelessly at both her daytime and nighttime jobs but always kept a smile on her face. Even after long days talking to college students, she saved the energy to tell fun and fascinating bedtime stories to her granddaughter and grandson about the goings-on of campus life. Some of her stories were about young, first-year college students who had found themselves homesick and would reach out to her for comfort. But most of her stories were about "the big game" that was to come or "the big game" that had just been.

Adelaide Miller, affectionately known as Mrs. Miller by the students, was my grandmother and my introduction to the University of Miami Hurricanes and its football program. She loved going to the games, she loved cheering on the team, and she loved being surrounded by fellow work associates and students out at the stadium. She truly bled green and orange.

I spent a good portion of my childhood talking about and playing football with my brother in our oversized green and orange T-shirts. My brother and I would don our University of Miami hand-me-downs and recruit other neighborhood children to join our team for the ultimate matchup... the Canes versus the Noles. The Canes typically won every game, of course, but sometimes those Noles gave us a run for our money.

As I became a teenager and later a University of Miami student myself, I still wore my orange and green, and continued the family tradition of supporting the Canes.

I remember fondly how, every morning, after seeing my brother and me off to school, my grandmother would drive the short distance to work in her cornflower-blue Rambler. She loved the beautiful drive to Ponce de Leon. The palm-tree–lined street was flanked by a plethora of bougainvillea, hibiscus, and liriope plants. "There is nothing like the tropics!" she would often declare. My grandmother would make a left hand turn and enter the school through the front entrance of the University of Miami and then continue making herself available to new generations of Hurricanes football fans.

2014 Northwestern University graduate Andrew Rothschild reflects on his experiences as a member of the Northwestern University Marching Band:

Every year at the end of the last home football game, the Northwestern University Marching Band has a tradition of celebrating its senior class by having the entire band, minus the seniors, line up on both sides of the field, forming a tunnel for the seniors to run onto Ryan Field, the university football field. The senior class then runs through the tunnel together as the rest of the band plays the school fight song. It was during this tradition that I learned something I didn't expect to learn from marching band, and consequently, my time in college.

My two greatest passions growing up were sports and music. This led me to participate in marching band, the perfect combination of sports and music. As a member of the marching band, I would get to play drums and be as close to Northwestern football as I could be without actually putting on football pads (I would last about two plays before my body would snap in half). Rooting for Northwestern football my entire life, I had always been very emotionally invested in how the team performed. Whenever the team won, I was ecstatic and filled with uncontrollable excitement. Losses, however, left me inconsolable. Although game days as a marching band member were a constant adrenaline rush from the moment I woke up at 6 a.m. until the game was over at 3 p.m., I always felt a lot worse at the end of losses, compared with wins.

My final home game was different. My fellow senior band mates and I were running through the tunnel the band had made for us, and we were all laughing and smiling. As the fight song played, I couldn't help but see the scoreboard as my friends and I ran across Ryan Field one final time. The scoreboard read, "Michigan State 30, Northwestern 6." Normally seeing something like this would wipe the smile immediately from my face, and I would spend the next few hours in my room sulking, contemplating the various things that Northwestern could have done better. As I looked around, however, I realized that I didn't feel the same pangs of disappointment that I usually felt after a loss. I was just happy I was still on the field, hanging out with my marching band friends one last time.

It took me until that moment to discover how much my time in Northwestern University Marching Band truly meant to me. I always thought the greatest reason I loved the marching band was because it combined Northwestern football with drumming. Northwestern University Marching Band was more than just a musical organization that played at football games. My experiences in the marching band centered on the people I met, the friends I made, and the camaraderie we formed over my 4 years in the group. If the marching band had been just about drumming and football, my last home game would be a bleak memory. I would have reflected only on how disappointing it was that my final home game was a blowout loss to Michigan State.

What I learned from this whole experience that I didn't expect was that happiness is driven by the people you surround yourself with, not necessarily by the activities you do. Telling people I wore a drum harness for two and a half hours a day for 4 months while practicing outside through rain, cold, and hail each year I was in college sounds like something only a masochist would do. Telling people I was in a group with 180 of my closest friends sounds a lot more enjoyable. What the marching band taught me was that as long as I was surrounded by driven, spirited, and positive people, I could be happy doing anything, even if it involved suffering another agonizing loss in football.

Another marching band member (but at Ohio University), Mindy Kay Smith, talks about what happened when the school lost power in 1996:

I was sitting alone in my room when the lights went out. I had just finished dinner, and I was enjoying the last of my chocolate soft serve cone in peace. I loved living in the same building as so many other marching band members. But sometimes a girl needs a little space.

When it first happened, I assumed it was something I had done. I didn't know what that could have been, but I thought of myself as a person who caused accidental power outages. I was, at the very least, a girl who set off fire alarms with microwave popcorn.

I waited for the lights to flicker back on. They did not. I looked out the window and saw that the streetlights were out as well. All of Athens was dark and still. I ventured out of my room a few steps, but it was even darker in the windowless hallway.

So I sat. All alone. Wondering where my roommate was. Soon enough there was a knock on the door. And there stood three of my marching band friends. Because that's the thing about the kind of friends you make in the Ohio University Marching 110. They may get on your nerves at times from sheer overexposure. But in times of trouble and confusion, they will come and find you.

I was told to grab my cymbals. The four of us knocked on two more doors to become eight. The eight of us, instruments in hand, spread out to other dorms. Before long, the marching band was giving an impromptu concert on the pitch-black college green.

I don't remember the exact cause of the blackout or how long the power was off. But I do remember the feeling I had while crashing my cymbals and dancing for my Bobcat community. And I think back to that night when I think of

64

Ohio University. I realize how important it is to attend a college where, when the lights go out, the students find each other on college green. Not to riot or loot. But to spend time together.

Opening My Mind

Dr. Aaron Kesselheim is Associate Professor of Medicine at Harvard Medical School/Brigham and Women's Hospital. He runs the Program On Regulation, Therapeutics, And Law, an interdisciplinary research group that studies intersections between public health law and health care delivery. Aaron began college with an interest in science and hoped to one day go to medical school. But he also enjoyed writing and history. At Harvard, he stumbled on to the history of science, which ended up shaping his career:

So I was walking around the Science Center at Harvard looking for the laboratory I was assigned to for my freshman introductory biology course, when I came across a door marked History of Science. Never before having heard of this as a formal discipline, I went through the door and found a labyrinth of offices that was actually a separate academic department housed at the Science Center.

That morning, I asked around about the courses offered and found that they sponsored their own concentration called "History and Science." I left to go to the lab with a newfound excitement that there was a discipline that seemed to straddle all of my interests.

My subsequent concentration in History and Science at Harvard basically introduced me to my career. I learned about the interconnectedness of science and society, and how cultural norms and other factors end up defining the search for facts and their interpretation. Allan Brandt, Bashi Sabra, John Murdoch, and other professors in the department helped move me from my interest in practicing medicine to more broadly understanding how laws and regulations affect how medicine is practiced in the United States.

By the end of college, I had decided to apply to law school as well as medical school so that I could help not just patients in front of me, but all patients, too. And now, that's exactly what we try to do in the research group I run.

Scott Breen, a 2011 graduate of Georgetown University and an attorney-advisor at the National Oceanic and Atmospheric Administration, explains what he did when he first learned that there was such a thing as environmental economics:

When I started college at Georgetown University, my true interest was still shrouded in haze, but then I heard the term that revealed my passions (or so I thought).

Forest ecology professor: "A seminal paper in environmental economics by Robert Costanza found the average value of the ecosystem services provided by the entire biosphere is 33 trillion dollars."

Me (in my head): "Whoa. That is a huge number! But wait. Did he just say environmental economics? There is a field where I can apply my interest in economics to my love of the environment?"

Hearing the term "environmental economics" kindled an inner fire. I had to learn more, so I decided I would research the term. I found the National Center for Environmental Economics (NCEE) at the U.S. Environmental Protection Agency, which was located only 3 miles from campus. That is the beauty of going to school in Washington, D.C.—wherever your interests take you, there is probably a national center for it, and you can get involved.

I played the student card. I emailed an economist at NCEE explaining that I was a student at Georgetown University, that I had just heard the term environmental economics, and that I would appreciate the opportunity to discuss his work. This economist was very gracious and agreed to meet with me at a coffee shop in Dupont Circle.

That coffee meeting turned into an introductory discussion regarding the importance of determining the benefits and costs of various environmental policies.

I was excited. I enrolled in an environmental economics class at Georgetown with another economist, and he asked if anyone in the class would be interested in a paid internship with NCEE. I jumped at the chance. My work touched on a variety of environmental issues and challenged me to do tasks and to grapple with concepts in economics that pushed the limits of my abilities. I grew from the experience.

Although I am not an economist today, it was through my experiences in the world of environmental economics that I realized the models, formulas, and assumptions did not fully energize me. However, the policies and laws behind what we were analyzing very much attracted my attention. I noted this and pivoted. I decided to pursue a joint law and public affairs degree at Indiana University. As of this writing, I am an environmental lawyer at the National Oceanic and Atmospheric Administration.

I say "as of this writing" purposely. I have already noted other interests in my life and can imagine myself pivoting yet again. However, there is no easier time to pivot and explore than during college. Listen when those fires inside you are kindled; then stoke them and do not let them burn out until you have learned from your experiences.

I am thankful that I stoked the environmental economics fire inside me because it helped me learn what I did not want to do and then helped me wind my way to the next stop in my journey.

Dr. James C. Goodloe IV, Presbyterian Minister and Executive Director, Foundation for Reformed Theology, reflects on his time as a Davidson College undergraduate:
In the spring of 1971, I graduated as valedictorian from Gallatin Senior High School in Gallatin, Tennessee. That

fall, I was a freshman at Davidson College in Davidson, North Carolina. Of the 25 young men on the first floor of Sentelle Hall, 18 of us had been valedictorians. I had landed in a different world.

I realized that high school had kept me off the streets until my education began. Typing and driver's education had been important. The math classes had been good. And what Coach Foster had taught us might have been most important of all. More of that in a moment. But I had arrived at Davidson to study ancient history, Greek philosophy, classical Greek, literature, art, logic, and on and on, and that was wonderful.

People went to high school because they had to. Literally. The law required it. Some appreciated and enjoyed learning, but others did not want to be there at all. They made that obvious.

Davidson was different. Every single student wanted to be there. Every student had asked to be there. Every student had applied to be there. And that made all the difference in the world. Everyone wanted to learn.

Now, back to Coach Foster. "There is never an assignment in this class," he said, as he handed out the chemistry books on the first day of our junior year. "By the same token, there is always an assignment." Not one of us knew what he meant.

The next day, he asked whether there were any questions on chapter one. No one moved, so he said, "Take out a clean sheet of paper, and we'll take the test on chapter one." Oh.

The day after that, he asked whether there were any questions on chapter two. A lot of hands went up, and mine may have been first. He answered our questions one by one. This went on for about a week, until one day there were no more questions on chapter two. Then we took that test.

This continued for the rest of the year, as we worked through the text. It could be argued that this track coach, required by law to teach classes, also had found a way to avoid preparing lesson plans. But that would miss the point.

What Coach Foster taught me, far beyond chemistry, was that my education was my responsibility, not his. And, in teaching me that, he fulfilled his responsibility many times over.

Coach Foster also helped me to navigate the strange new world in which I had landed. Davidson was grueling far beyond anything I had ever done. By the end of my 4 years, I felt that I had learned enough that if I could have done it all again, I really could have benefited from it.

That, of course, was the point. No, I had not learned everything I would ever need to know. Not by a long shot. But I had learned how to study. I had learned how to work. And I had learned how to learn. So my education was not just the content of my courses, as delightful as that was, but even more importantly, the method of learning. I had learned enough not only to go on to seminary and graduate school but also to embark upon a lifetime of learning.

Thank you, Coach Foster. And thank you, Davidson College. You served me well.

Joseph Coci, a graduate of the University of Virginia and now president of Mountain Development Corporation in Connecticut, discusses the value of his philosophy degree:

I had the good fortune to attend the University of Virginia. I applied for the 2-year honors program in philosophy at the recommendation of one of my friends who was in the program. This program was modeled after the English tutorial method of teaching used at Oxford and Cambridge.

Each semester was dedicated to one of the major fields in philosophy: epistemology, metaphysics, ethics, and moral philosophy. I was assigned to one professor each semester. I had no classes other than elective classes in unrelated fields that were of interest to me, and one weekly tutorial with my assigned professor. Each week, my professor would give me a lengthy reading list on a given topic. I was expected to write a 15-page analysis of that topic based on my studies. On Monday evenings, I would present the paper to my professor, and the next day during the tutorial, he would grill me on everything in the paper, including my understanding of the topic, writing style, grammar, and logic.

During my 2-year major, I read works by many of the major philosophers, including Plato, Aristotle, Kant, Socrates, Wittgenstein, Bentham, Aquinas, and Descartes. I was particularly drawn to epistemology, which is the study of the limits of the human mind, the study of knowledge versus belief, how we know what we know, and the power of mind over body.

My studies in philosophy, particularly epistemology, gave me the ability to think critically and logically, and to reason through problems or issues. I use these analytical skills every day in my business career. For example, several years ago, I was working to structure a complex real estate transaction involving a property in bankruptcy with a convoluted ownership structure and warring parties. My training in philosophy enabled me to prioritize the issues and to achieve a solution that was satisfactory to the seller of the property, the bankruptcy court, and to my partners as the purchasing entity.

My education in philosophy has given me a better understanding of the world and our humanity. I often reflect on issues raised during my studies. For example, is there proof of the existence of God? While there are no definitive answers to many of these questions and debates about these issues have raged on for centuries, the study of philosophy has given me a sense of wonder about ourselves as human beings and about our place in the universe.

Laura Hendricks is a business administration graduate of Ohio University whose life was changed by a magazine she read while in college. Laura is now a farmer and co-owner of Alaskan Wilderness Experience and Denali Organic Growers in Healy, Alaska (population 1,021):

It all started with an issue of *Outside Magazine* when I was a junior in college. I was studying business administration, and spring break was upon me.

My original plans of basking in the Florida sun had fallen through, as can be the case when one is faced with little money and poorly developed planning skills. So, on this fateful day, I was in Cleveland, waiting for my dad to fix the drain on a rental property.

In hindsight, I was waiting for my life to unfold.

With time to kill, I casually reached over to the coffee table and picked up an issue of *Outside Magazine*. Time seemed to stand still. I was broadsided by a world I didn't know existed. I was drawn deeper into the photos, the articles, and the idea of a reality far from what I knew.

I remember the feeling that came over me. The feeling that life had just gotten bigger, that I had just touched on something that made me feel more alive, more vibrant, more passionate than, say, calculus. I shared this with my father.

Three days later, it was my birthday. Dad, being the wise soul that he is, must have recognized that this new seed might need some nurturing in taking root. Off to the outdoor store we went, where he helped me pick out my first tent. And, for good measure, he threw in a Swiss army knife and that same issue of *Outside Magazine*.

I read that magazine, cover to cover, and I mean cover to cover. In the very back of the issue I saw a classified ad for summer trip leaders.

My curiosity was piqued. What is a summer trip leader? Could I be one? I decided to call the number in the ad. I learned that the positions were "pretty much filled" but that they would send along a brochure to help me better understand the program.

The brochure arrived with glossy pages of kids rock climbing, canoeing, rafting, hiking, and backpacking. My thoughts kept coming back to doing all of this. Do people really get paid to do this? My heart was racing, and my blood was pumping.

I knew that positions were "pretty much filled." To me, that meant there was a sliver of hope. That's all I needed, that's all we ever need. More than anything I had ever wanted, I wanted that job. I wanted to experience more of that feeling!

I knew full well that I didn't have a lick of experience. I also knew I couldn't fully sell myself on paper or a phone interview. I had to stack the odds in my favor and win the position with motivation, determination, and personality. So I loaded up my car and drove 8 hours to have a personal interview.

I got the job!

What I discovered that summer was that I was far more capable than I had ever dreamed. I was perfectly at home sleeping under the stars and helping others to connect with Mother Nature while reflecting more deeply about their relationships. I learned to feed my soul with ideas and possibilities.

I came to appreciate the importance of understanding the relationship between the outdoors and our precious bodies. I discovered our bodies' ability to communicate through subtle cues—we just have to learn to listen. When we learn to listen, we know without a doubt what turns to take and what doors to open. We do a service to ourselves, to our communities, and ultimately, to the world when we create a life with our personal signature on it, a life that makes our hearts sing!

My husband and I now own and operate (utilizing my business degree) Alaskan Wilderness Experience and Denali Organic Growers, an awesome off-the-grid small-scale organic farm and learning center. Each year, we bring on a new group of interns, and we enhance one another's lives as we share the journey from seed to harvest of plants, ideas, and dreams.

2004 University of Dallas graduate Matt F. explains how excited he became in college when he first learned about the field of psychology. His understanding of psychology helped him as a professional soccer referee and continues to enrich his life:

Out of sheer curiosity, I took an introductory psychology course during my sophomore year at the University of Dallas. I had little to no exposure to the subject and was already three semesters deep into a pre-medicine track. But that one psychology course convinced me to change majors.

I remember the opening lecture: The professor, who was also chair of the psychology department, gave a captivating introduction to the subject. To explain the value of studying animal behavior, he morphed into his version of a bonobo, a species of chimpanzee that shares 99% of human DNA. He grunted and knuckle-walked around the lecture hall while explaining what studying bonobos has revealed about human communication and behavior. Next, he discussed the tension between existentialism and determinism in modern psychology. I loved it. By the end of the hour, I knew I had to change my major.

I ended up graduating with a bachelor's in psychology. I still have all of my college psychology books, and I look over them regularly.

College is not merely a means to an end—a degree or a job. It is an opportunity to discover and explore passions you didn't even know you had. As a former professional soccer referee, I never worked full time in the field of psychology. But my time spent studying perception, motivation, and the meaning we ascribe to experience has forever informed my understanding of my life and that of others.

Stephanie Scherpf, co-founder of the Boston dance company Jean Appolon Expressions, shares how her senior thesis at the University of Virginia—and her love for the work of Toni Morrison—helped develop and construct her own identity:

I was accepted into the English Department's Distinguished Majors Program, which required a senior thesis. Heading into my senior year at the University of Virginia, I had enough credits so that I was able to take the first semester off to focus solely on my thesis. Toni Morrison had won the Nobel Prize in Literature in 1993, and I was in love with her books. The year before, I had even sought out a Toni Morrison Conference at Bellarmine University in Louisville, Kentucky.

Back at UVA, I dove into researching my thesis. I remember doing a library search for literary criticism on Morrison and finding Morrison's own master's thesis written at Cornell University in 1955—*Virginia Woolf's and William Faulkner's Treatment of the Alienated.* Woolf was another author I read closely. Her books had become cornerstones of my growing feminist library. The Distinguished Majors Program required an essay of 50 pages, but I ended up writing 100 under the title of "The Critical Dialogue Between Toni Morrison and Virginia Woolf on Reconstructing the Female Self." I paired books by Morrison and Woolf and put them in conversation with each other: *Playing in the Dark* and *A Room of One's Own*; *Sula* and *Mrs. Dalloway*; and *Jazz* and *To the Lighthouse.* What emerged was a close analysis of the literature of two women who I posited "reached across barriers of time, race and culture to engage in a dialogue about female identity."

Twenty years later, I realize that imagining a critical dialogue between Toni Morrison and Virginia Woolf was as much my first major foray into the world of literary criticism as it was about helping me construct my own identity as a soon-to-be college graduate.

In retrospect, the thesis project helped me find out who I was in the world and what role I wanted to play in it. Following graduation from UVA, I enrolled in a Ph.D. program for literature at the University of Washington where I focused on how literature and cultural studies could be change agents in the classroom. I thought if literature could change me, why couldn't it change others and ultimately, the world? Although I chose to leave academia after finishing my master's and start a career in managing arts for social change programs, I will always consider my senior thesis project at UVA as seminal in forming the woman I am today.

Chris Svoboda graduated from Sweet Briar College in 1984. She reflects on her first student-alumnae lacrosse game and the feelings that fueled the successful effort in 2015 to save Sweet Briar from being closed:

During the spring semester of my junior year, the varsity lacrosse team had to play an exhibition game, on a Saturday, against the alums. This was the first year such a thing would take place and we all had to participate to show team and school spirit. Ugh!

I was in my goalie gear dreading the warm-up, the game, and the old ladies. Then time seemed to stand still as a beautiful red convertible Alfa Romeo came roaring toward the field, with a bunch of alums piled in with their gear overflowing, laughing and screaming. And then everything changed. The alums were cool. Who knew?

We had a blast that weekend, and this was the start of a new tradition that continues to this day. Every spring, we take a pilgrimage back to The Briar and are taken back in time. The planning begins in December with a group of alumnae coordinating travel, lodging, and other activities. Some amazingly talented graphic artists design commemorative T-shirts and these T-shirts then become cherished prizes for those who play.

I am proud to say that alumnae lacrosse players were among the first to rise up after the announcement of Sweet Briar's closing.

Citing insurmountable financial challenges, the board of directors of Sweet Briar College voted on February 28, 2015, to close the school. When I first read about this, I thought it was a joke. But within minutes my phone, email and Facebook were blowing up. The board was close-lipped.

Alums, faculty, and students were heartbroken, dismayed, and let down by representatives who had given no warning. A previous president, who moved on, had left us with assurances that all was fine. Yet 6 months later, quite the opposite was true. As far as we knew, no one had approached alums for assistance in figuring out how to turn the college's future around.

Within a week, our network had interwoven itself on Facebook, and we decided we were collectively going to get to the bottom of this and keep the school open. Intimate meetings took place on campus, in nearby Amherst, on Capitol Hill, on the phone, and all around the world.

It's hard to completely capture why we SBC alums love our school so much and return to campus at every opportunity. Perhaps it is the number of times the school has ranked in the top 10 of most beautiful campuses in the United States, or because of the quality of student life and student/faculty interactions. The campus is paradise—more than 3,500 acres of serene woodlands and rolling hills at the foot of the Blue Ridge Mountains. A boathouse that is frozen in time sits on the edge of one of two lakes. Horses roam through fields and minds are free to think and dream.

In my class of fewer than 150 students, five of us were daughters of the Class of 1960, which had fewer than 100 in the class. We had all visited the campus with our mothers over the years, and I never doubted I would end up at SBC.

A Sweet Briar affiliation is a key that unlocks just about any door that you would want it to. Some alum knows someone somewhere who can make it happen for you. Wherever I have traveled in the world, I have been able to find alums nearby who are more than willing to give me an intro or a backstory. All it takes is a quick email to the alumnae office and almost instantaneously, they respond with a list of alumnae contacts.

Even when the old administration tried to cut off our connection to the alumnae office in hopes of stalling our disseminating the information about Saving Sweet Briar, some tech-savvy alums were able to access the rolls.

As most people now know, we were able to save the school. It is going to be better in its new future than it would have been if the status quo had remained, and the majority of alums had just taken it for granted and not gotten involved. But luckily there was a shakeup, and we dug in, spending sleepless days and nights for the cause.

We will never know the real reason for trying to shut down the school. The land is extremely valuable, of course, but it is more valuable to the students, alums, staff, faculty, and parents. I began to understand just how special and valuable Sweet Briar is during our very first student-alumnae lacrosse game in the '80s.

Jeff Spicher is director of the HealthCircle Primary Care Clinic at the University of Colorado Colorado Springs. In 1994, he received the Outstanding Faculty Practice Award from the National Organization of Nurse Practitioner Faculties. He shares how he decided to become a nurse:

Perhaps the most important lesson I learned was during the time when I was between college and graduate school. I graduated from Eastern Mennonite University with a biology education degree and discovered that I did not want to teach at the high school level and could not do much with my bachelor's in biology. I had just dropped out of a master's program in environmental sciences at the University of Virginia and was working as a laboratory technician for an elderly physics professor.

I was searching for what I wanted to do with my life and was spending a great deal of time trying to figure out what my passion was and what I might be good at. I spent a lot of time in prayer and reflection, evaluating my skills and what I ultimately wanted to do that would reflect my personal convictions and worldview.

After months of soul searching and frequent sleepless nights, I was awoken one night and had a very strong sense that I was supposed to become a nurse. This was conveyed to me through a feeling, an answer to my questioning. The feeling was overwhelming and, at the same time, oddly comforting. I felt at peace and warm all over, like someone had wrapped me in a blanket that had just been taken out of the dryer. I embraced the idea and was able to sleep that night, my first good night's sleep in a long while.

In the morning, I told my wife that I was going to become a nurse. She laughed and thought I was crazy. She then asked me if I was just doing this because she was in nursing school at the time. I relayed my story to her and told her that I felt sure that this was a calling for me and that this was my life's work. This all happened in 1992 and since then, I have become a family nurse practitioner and a college professor and have never regretted my decision to enter the nursing profession. My hope is that I can inspire others to follow their passions, not only in nursing but also in life, and to listen to the still small voice in all of us.

The Unexpected

Award-winning Los Angeles screenwriter and University of Massachusetts Amherst graduate Dode Levenson explains how he almost didn't go to college:

Surprisingly, I almost didn't go to college. My parents were both educators with advanced degrees, so my decision came as quite a shock. My reasoning was straightforward. University tuition cost a fortune; I was one of four children; my parents weren't Rockefellers; and I didn't see how a degree would help me make money in real estate—which is where I saw my future. I was a willful young man of 18 and I couldn't imagine my parents saying anything that would change my mind.

I braced myself for a confrontation that never happened. Once my father saw my determination, instead of being angry, he sat me down and told me a story about his first year in college. As a liberal arts major, he was forced to take a science class and chose Astronomy. In my mind I was already yawning. He told me how he felt when he first walked into that class and saw the magic of the cosmos, etc.

I remained unmoved.

Did he harbor some secret fascination with planets, comets, and the movement of celestial objects? Did he think I had any interest in those subjects or in becoming an astronomer?

He smiled and said the lesson wasn't about whether or not to become an astronomer. The lesson was about a world of possible careers that he had never even considered up until the moment he walked into that freshman Astronomy class.

He said he would respect my decision but simply didn't want me to go through life as a real estate mogul without at least exploring the possibility that there might be a field of interest I hadn't fathomed, especially one that I might fall in love with, given the opportunity.

Hard to argue with that. After our discussion, to my mother's relief, I agreed to go to college—but insisted on going to a state school with a reasonable tuition. There I discovered my love of writing and made enduring friendships at the college newspaper—which I treasure to this day. Eventually, I left a promising career in journalism to pursue a life in the creative arts, settling in Los Angeles and becoming a screenwriter. If you talk to me about real estate today, my eyes will probably glaze over.

How's that for an unexpected lesson? (Thanks, Dad!)

James Minichello is a graduate of the University of South Carolina and director of communications for AASA, The School Superintendents Association. He writes about a locked door on campus that taught him valuable lessons about being on time and preparing in advance:

Business calendars are filled with scheduled meetings that include dates, times, phone numbers to call, places to be, and the subjects of these meetings.

While attending a college journalism class at the University of South Carolina, I learned that if a job interview begins at 11:00 a.m., the time to arrive at the person's office is no later than 10:30 a.m. This time can be equally as important as the skills you bring to a position. The extra time provides you with the ability to compose yourself, take a few deep breaths, have a cup of coffee, gather your thoughts, review key messages, and make sure your tie is straight.

I learned the 30-minute rule during a broadcast newswriting course with Professor Lee Dudek. Some might have labeled Dr. Dudek as old school. However, the lifelong lessons I learned from him have been invaluable to me as a broadcast journalist and public relations professional. Bravo to Dr. Dudek and old school.

Dr. Dudek locked the classroom door only a few seconds after our 11:30 a.m. class was scheduled to begin. His reasoning was simple and made a ton of sense: "When you're on the air and the red light goes on, you need to already be seated comfortably in the anchor's chair and reviewing copy," he would later tell beleaguered students who stood at the door unable to attend class because of tardiness. Two days after the semester started, nobody was late again.

Indirectly, Dr. Dudek was priming his students to become professional broadcasters. He encouraged students who couldn't be on time to "find something else to do." Hence, I learned one of the most important lessons in journalism—if you're serious about making a career in journalism, no matter if it's print or broadcast, remember that deadlines are deadlines.

Dr. Dudek also encouraged us to not cram the night before a test. He suggested that we study periodically throughout the week (or more, if necessary), and go to the movies the night before. Sounded simple.

Today, when it comes to a major project at work, I try to have the project completed at least 1 or 2 days before it's due. I use the remaining time productively to review the piece of writing, video, etc., and then make any needed tweaks or edits. Because of my schedule, I don't get to see many movies anymore, but the message is to find something to do that helps you relax.

In addition, it can take a day or two after the first draft of an assignment to be able to come back to it with fresh eyes. The day or two provides me with an opportunity to review the material, not only as a writer, but also from the perspective of someone reading it for the first time.

Building in extra time is critical because it can help avoid mistakes. Sometimes it may take four or five read throughs—after you've completed an assignment—to pinpoint another word or phrase that could provide more clarity or style to the assigned work.

I try to follow the lessons that I learned from Dr. Dudek for every meeting and assignment. Sounds old school, but good things and good advice forever keep their value.

Karen Rindge is a graduate of the University of North Carolina at Chapel Hill. She shares how her college experience led her to Zimbabwe and back to North Carolina:

I'm from a small town in the mountains of North Carolina. Growing up, our family never discussed politics or public policy. When I was accepted into the University of North Carolina at Chapel Hill, I had no idea my college experience would eventually steer me on a path around the globe, or that my eyes would be opened to dramatically different cultures and perspectives on how the world ought to function.

I had a hunch of my yearnings, however, and selected a political science major that soon both pulled me out of my comfort zone while connecting me deeper into my heart. College lectures and debates among political science students with varying standpoints expanded my awareness and challenged me to consider what was true for me. I recall experiencing what literally felt like my parts of my brain stretching and new synapses firing in my head.

As I began to explore public policy, I was inspired to express my developing political views and participated in rallies in UNC's famous "Pit." The notion that individual expression of views (no matter right or left on the spectrum) was not only permitted, but also encouraged, thrilled me.

This was the '80s, and the South African anti-apartheid movement was flowing across college campuses. My senior year, I found my voice in the student anti-apartheid organization. We rallied in the Pit for UNC divestment, and appealed to the Board of Trustees to withdraw from corporations doing business in South Africa. We built a shanty outside the administration building, and I'll never forget the sadness, shame, and irony of watching campus service employees following orders to tear down the shanty built by privileged college students.

I had never traveled outside the United States and Canada, but my journey had already begun. Later, after working in Washington, D.C. in the U.S. House of Representatives, when I had the chance to apply for a Rotary Foundation international postgraduate scholarship, I knew where I wanted to go—Southern Africa. UNC's anti-apartheid student leader was from Zimbabwe, and from him I had gotten the bug to explore deeper. In 1989, my college experience expanded to being a minority white student at the University of Zimbabwe, where textbooks were extremely scarce, and lectures delivered an African point of view. Visiting South Africa, I felt discomfort traveling in the apartheid system and actually observing its impact on real people rather than studying it theoretically.

After studying development policy from a Zimbabwean perspective, I knew my career path would be linked to my experiences. I concluded that the most beneficial task I could do to help improve the lives of Africans was to influence U.S. foreign policy affecting international development. Living in Southern Africa helped prepare me for a career in advocacy promoting U.S. foreign aid for international reproductive health care and women's rights. Returning to Washington, I had the good fortune to land nonprofit jobs in the international divisions of both Planned Parenthood Federation of America and the National Wildlife Federation. I also became an international advocate at several United Nations conferences striving for rights, health care, sustainability, and equity. Connecting with advocates from many Southern nations continued my journey, which paradoxically also pointed me back to the critical

84

importance of what the U.S. does to affect the rest of the world.

Without a doubt, my college experiences had a profound impact on me, and will be in my soul for the rest of my life. From the mountains of North Carolina to the townships and savanna of Southern Africa, I'll never see the world quite the same. And now, back in North Carolina's capital city, my family and children discuss politics all the time.

University of Texas graduate Sandeep Seth explains the road that took him from New York to Texas:

I was never supposed to go to the college that I attended, which was the University of Texas at Austin. I was supposed to go to Boston University.

You see, my family had moved from India to New York, and that was the American culture that I grew up with from age 5 until my senior year of high school. In the middle of my senior year of high school, my father was transferred to Houston, and my parents did not want me to stay back in New York, though several of my friends' parents offered to have me stay the remainder of the year with them.

So we moved. In the course of that move, out went BU and in came UT, which also had an aerospace engineering program.

Texas was different. In fact, I would say that the move to Texas when I was a 17-year-old New Yorker was more of a cultural change than the move to New York from New Delhi was when I was a 5-year-old. I expected that everybody in Texas got around on horsepower. And they did, though it was mostly in groups of 350 horsepower under the hood of a pickup truck. The cowboy hats and boots were real. Folks wore them. There were real ranchers and oilmen (well, mostly oilmen, but some oil women too) and cowboys and cowgirls. Country and western music actually existed, and folks went out to clubs to ride mechanical bulls and dance to "Cotton-Eyed Joe."

It was incredible, for I was every bit a Yankee. And although Houston was a big city, it felt like a small town and people were different. They were friendlier, in some ways, in an easygoing way. I made some new Texas friends, but I always had one eye looking back to the depth of my New York relationships. On some level, I was always making a comparison.

I had visited Austin only briefly, so I didn't really have a feel for it when I moved there. As with most students, I was both anxious and excited. The majority culture in Austin for me was intriguing. You see, for Texas, most of the brightest folks from the Texas student pool who don't want to go out-of-state go to UT Austin.

There was a vibe to the place, a coolness, you might say, that was wild and musical and also liberal, and yet rooted in Texas folksiness. If Austin were a person, it would be Stevie Ray Vaughan. If Austin were a type of music, it would be his music. I had no problem at all adapting to that. Even though the engineering workload was massive and stressful, I enjoyed the vibe of Austin's culture. In fact, it came fairly easily.

In my few philosophy classes, taken in equal parts for personal interest and to break the monotony of the engineering curriculum, I found that there was an intellectual tradition to UT that had its own history and style. For instance, there was a high-quality level of discussion that could be made in an easygoing and humble style, often over shared barbeque, beer, and beans (always, of course, with raw jalapeno and onions on the side). I loved this part of Austin, and it helped to soothe a transplanted New Yorker (who was really out of his element and in some ways shattered from the relocation), even if I didn't have the history in Texas to get fully inside of it.

The Unexpected

Dr. Linda Scherr, Dean of Arts and Sciences at Middlesex County College, shares a formative experience from her senior year at Cornell University that helped her realize her path would be in academia:

A few weeks into the fall semester of my senior year at Cornell University, Dan sat next to me in Art History lecture and said, "I missed class on Tuesday. Can I copy your notes?" I had sat with Dan and Kathy throughout the semester and he knew I never missed class and that I took thorough notes (and I still do today). It was one of my favorite classes—a survey of Renaissance and Baroque art taught by an incredibly charismatic, energetic professor. I still think back to that class today and can picture the auditorium and conjure the images of my favorite works of Vermeer and Georges de La Tour.

I happily gave Dan my notes. A few days later, he and Kathy asked if I wanted to study with them for the upcoming midterm. I said I would, but added casually that I wasn't actually taking the class. Rather, I was sitting in for fun because I had a free period.

Dan and Kathy were amazed. They had never heard of auditing and had trouble grasping the idea that a 20-year-old would voluntarily attend more classes than required for graduation. I was almost equally amazed that they didn't see the unique opportunity that the Cornell University undergraduate course catalog offered. One could, essentially, study anything she wanted. Who wouldn't take advantage of that?

I doubt that that moment was memorable for Dan and Kathy (although I did study with them and both did well in the course), but it was a formative experience for me. I understood with a certainty I had never before experienced that my path would be in academia. I couldn't imagine not being in a place where I was surrounded by intellectually curious people whose views on lifelong learning were kindred with mine.

I later pursued a Ph.D. in Ancient History at the University of Pennsylvania (where I continued to audit courses outside my major) and now am a community college administrator. Every day, I am engaged in the work of helping students find their paths inside and outside of academia. And I continue to learn—from my colleagues and, on the best of days, from my students.

Nick Noble, host of the Folk Revival radio show on New England's WICN, shares a conversation he had during his first night at Trinity College that led to four years of participation in a campus singing group:

I was one week late for the start of my freshman year in college because I had a summer job that didn't end on time (and I needed the money). So when I got to campus, I had missed orientation and didn't know many people there at all. On my first night, I was walking along the main campus, wondering what I was going to do with myself and how I was going to fit in, when I ran into a senior whom I had known a little bit from church back home.

"Great to see you!" she said. "Are you going to the concert?"

"What concert?" I asked.

It turns out that the campus singing group was giving its first performance to start the school year.

"You like to sing," she told me. "Check it out."

So I did. I found my way to the concert hall, which was packed. The only room anywhere was at the very front, sitting on the floor, practically at the feet of the performers (six men, six women, two guitars, and an upright bass). I really enjoyed the show, and when it was over, the performers announced that, since half of them were recent graduates back only to help out with the show that night, they would be holding auditions for new places in the group right after the concert.

88

Having nothing else to do, I went to the audition. I never thought I would get in. At least forty other students were auditioning for maybe five spots. But I got called back, and the second time there were a dozen of us. I made it.

I sang with that group for all four years of my college career. Through the group, I met members of the fraternity that I later joined. I made lifelong friends. And I had a home away from home.

I could have shrugged my shoulders that first night and either gone looking for a mindless party or just gone back to my room and fallen asleep. Instead, I checked out a concert, and within a week, I was part of something special.

Singer, songwriter, and recording artist Phil Rosenthal was a student in English literature at the University of Chicago. His long-standing interest in music led him to U. of C.'s Folk Society. Phil shares a story from his sophomore year:

Music has been at the center of my mind since I was pretty young. It started with Pete Seeger, when I was 5 or 6. I stumbled onto bluegrass a few years later, and spent many teenage hours listening to Bill Monroe, the Stanley Brothers, and Reno and Smiley, but my all-time favorites were Lester Flatt, Earl Scruggs, and the Foggy Mountain Boys. I travelled to several early festivals and was thrilled to hear many of these bands in person, but when I started my freshman year at the University of Chicago, in 1966, Flatt and Scruggs had eluded me.

U. of C.'s Folk Society brought a variety of performers and styles of music to the annual Folk Festival held in Mandel Hall each year. I became a member, mainly to be able to hang around backstage at the festival, especially with the bluegrass band hired for that year. My sophomore year, it was Flatt and Scruggs! A major snowstorm hit Chicago the day before the festival, but Scruggs, a licensed pilot, flew the band in with his small plane. I was waiting at Mandel

Hall for their arrival. I had offered to help them carry their instruments to the university housing where they would spend the night. I'll never forget carrying Earl's banjo, and turning my head every once in a while to make sure Earl was doing all right on the icy, snowy sidewalk.

A few hours later, it was time for their concert. I was in the room downstairs below the Mandel stage, standing quietly to the side as the band members took their instruments out, checked their tuning, and ran through a few songs. They were my favorite bluegrass band, then and now. It was a style they helped develop and refine. Their music, in that fairly large room, was laid back, effortless, and relaxed. And it sounded so much better in person than even on their classic Mercury and Columbia recordings! It had power, but ease to it as well. Those few minutes had a profound influence on me, and helped shape the music I would play from then on.

There were other organizations I joined at U. of C. that also influenced me greatly. Doc Films introduced me to films and directors I might never have discovered on my own (my first viewing of *Citizen Kane* was almost as exciting and influential as meeting Flatt and Scruggs). James O'Reilly directed me in several plays produced by the Court Theatre on campus. I got to know and play music with other bluegrass-obsessed musicians. And there were professors whose courses I enjoyed—Ned Rosenheim, Norman Maclean, Bruno Bettelheim, Edward Wasiolek. But my most memorable moments were those I spent with Lester and Earl and the Foggy Mountain Boys.

Nura Sadeghpour, a 2003 graduate of the University of California, Berkeley, reflects on a statistics final and the thirst for knowledge:

It was just a few hours before my statistics final that would count for more than half my grade. I was ready. I was about to rock a quick review of the material in the place that inspired me the most—at the wooden tables in the nook lined by glass windows of the International House Café, with a view of the San Francisco Bay. I had organized my statistics binder in logical fashion, from the introductory basic concepts of the course to the more complex ones introduced in class. I had prepped each section by providing context to the equations and theories that followed, literally and colloquially writing a story for myself in the top margins: "Here is why these formulas and concepts you are about to review for the class final are important. When you want to figure out the odds of a shark attack occurring near you, you will need to understand this number. Why? Let me tell you..."

My classmate sat across from me. We both had ice-blended mochas. I was happy. I understood it all. I didn't necessarily sign up for the class thinking I would, but as the weeks went by—applied math, got it. Math with a purpose? I'm in. In fact, of the four quizzes we had taken to date, I had scored 95%-100% on all of them; one had been used as an example in class.

The irony was that I didn't even have to take a statistics course. I was a communications major with an English minor. But I had told myself that this semester I wanted to diversify the mind, introduce a challenge, and prove to myself I had breadth—all of which I was doing very nicely. And now I was a gleeful double agent. The fact that the final would count as half my grade didn't phase me at all.

Until it did. Practically humming to myself, I opened my binder and began skimming through "Chapter 1." Then I just blanked. I remember that the walls immediately closed in on me—I had never understood what that even meant. My mind was a black hole and inside I was shaking.

When my friend asked what was wrong, I noticed that my hands were shaking too, uncontrollably, as I turned the pages. Suddenly, none of it was familiar. The stories I had created to explain the logical mathematical concepts that, just a week earlier, I used to explain to classmates had no meaning. It was a foreign language to me. I didn't remember anything. I struggled to read through a problem, and asked my friend to explain it to me.

My friend reminded me calmly, "Nura, you know this, you really know this."

But all I could say was, "No, nothing."

My whole body was shaking now, my friend was visibly distressed, and though I spoke in a slow and steady, almost monotone voice, almost patiently explaining to her that I no longer understood any of this, the panic inside me was visceral. This is how I walked into the auditorium of 400 people, and this is how I walked out, after having written minor thoughts and random made-up formulas on three of the six multifaceted questions. The other three questions I left blank.

I got an F on that final. A low, low F. My final grade in the class was a C. I remember asking myself weeks later why I had chosen to take the statistics class for a letter grade instead of just units, which wouldn't have affected my GPA. Taking a class I didn't need to take to expand my mind: commendable. Taking it for a grade when I didn't need to: questionable. A breakdown an hour before a test: gradeless.

Reflecting years later on this experience that punched me in the face from some dark corner of my mind, I still don't know what happened. But what it does provide for me is an extreme example of how grades do not always reflect learning, or even a student's motivation to learn. In a world that is increasingly interactive and creative in its spaces for minds to meet, qualitative and quantitative measures of learning might be expanding too. We see some professors, and some colleges, striking a balance between intrinsic and extrinsic motivation. I wonder how much further we can go in finding out how to make the thirst for knowledge the key thing to measure, to grade, paired with the actions and results that follow, rather than just the result itself—a "grade" that doesn't always tell the whole story.

Temple University graduate Shelly Beaser shares how college can offer students a chance to be part of a changing world—which happens to be how she met her husband:

I went to Temple University because I could afford it. Applications cost money, which I didn't have. I knew I could get into Temple. My high school GPA was very high and I knew I could work and afford Temple's $450 per semester. I could live at home and ride the bus, elevated, and subway to get there. According to my parents, sleep-away school wasn't for people like us. Everyone I met at Temple was a commuter and had at least one job. One of my friends described college choice as, "I could go to Temple on the subway or I could go to Temple on the bus."

I was a political science major. I loved the topic, and, since I was often one of very few women in the class, it was a dating-rich environment. I hadn't dated in high school, and in those days, and in my community, marriage was supposed to happen by the time a girl was 25. Therefore, not only was I expected to get a degree, but I was also expected to find a husband.

I dated a lot of wonderful men and wished that one of them might one day be my husband, but I wasn't finding anyone with whom I could imagine spending my life. One day, in the Temple newspaper, there was an ad for a computer dating service—Operation Match. What a crazy and novel idea. We used the college computer for research— carefully punching out cards filled with information and handing them over to the lab-coated grad students who would run the data.

A young man in one of my classes (who had been asking me out to no avail) showed me the ad and said we should each send in the questionnaire. He was certain we would be matched. I was certain we would not, but it sounded like fun. For $3.00 (I was earning $1.50 an hour), the ad promised that a list of names would arrive by mail.

It was a lengthy questionnaire to be filled out twice—once how I would answer the question, once how I wanted my date to answer the question. Then I got to weight each answer as to how important I thought it was to be matched on that characteristic.

I can't remember all of my responses but I know I wanted someone who was an A student, who was politically involved, studied history or government, and liked folk music.

When the list of matches arrived, I waited for the boys to call—and they did! Suddenly, I was meeting people who weren't from Philadelphia. These boys lived on campuses like Penn or Haverford and came from exotic places like New York or Boston or Washington. It was fun and I enjoyed first dates and even second dates with many of them. But there was one from Penn who was really special! I married him a year after graduation, and we have been together for almost 50 years.

Political consultant Peter Waldheim reflects on campus protests at the University of Wisconsin-Milwaukee after students were killed at Kent State University:

On May 4, 1970, Ohio National Guardsmen shot and killed four students, while wounding nine others on the Kent State campus. Some were taking part in anti-war protests, while others were simply walking to classes.

The shootings at Kent State fueled deepening public concerns about the war at a time when polls showed that a majority of Americans had turned against the war two years earlier. The war was particularly unpopular on American campuses, due, in part, to the reality that thousands of young people were still being drafted every month and sent to Vietnam (virtually every student at that time had friends or relatives who were serving in the Armed Forces in Vietnam).

In the wake of the shooting, protests exploded on campuses across the country.

"On strike, shut it down!" became the rallying cry of a potent coalition of anti-war forces committed to forcing institutions of higher learning throughout the United States to close in protest. The University of Wisconsin-Milwaukee campus, where I attended classes, was one of the hundreds that would have buildings seized, shut down, or in our case, both.

Two moments, in particular, have always remained with me.

As hundreds of student protesters gathered outside the university library demanding it be shut down, Professor "Manny" Gottlieb—probably 60-some years old, with a global reputation for his work in economics—stood alone in front of the doors, begging those assembled to reconsider. His lonely opposition was so striking that those in the crowd lowered their voices as he recounted how Hitler's goons had destroyed free thought in Germany by first eliminating access to books containing ideas they disliked.

"Please don't cut off access to books," he implored.

Although it was apparent that many (probably a majority) were moved by what he said, the "mob mentality" was such that the students ended up moving into the building and shutting it down.

On a less radical plane, students seized the Student Union and many began sleeping there. Protestors wasted no time proclaiming their ownership of the new "egalitarian community" they had inaugurated. In fact, in the first hour or so, a group of student protestors made signs proclaiming "People's Liberation Bathrooms," which they taped over every door sign that had previously designated simply "Men" or "Women."

Alas, it is one thing to proclaim a new utopian community—even if it would only be held for a couple of days before the police moved in—but another to get your new student citizenry to avail themselves fully of your offerings. I was acting as a go-between for the university administration and the protest leadership, and was in and out of the building at all times of the day and night for the few days that it was held. Nevertheless, I didn't see a single instance in which even the most radical protestor would buck tradition and go to any newly liberated bathroom that hadn't previously been solely dedicated to his or her own gender.

I guess there are some steps that were just too radical for the contemporary versions of "Che" and "Madame Defarge" then on display on the UWM campus.

Clay Eals, author of Every Time a Bell Rings: The Wonderful Life of Karolyn Grimes *and* Steve Goodman: Facing the Music, *shares how his most meaningful college experiences occurred in the nighttime:*

The best things in life often happen at night. This may sound counter-intuitive, because the light of day symbolizes hope and new beginnings. At the same time, there is something indefinably life-giving in the relative silence and intimacy of night. Thwarting the typical social cycles and "going the extra mile" in darkness can transcend the need for rest, embed deep insights, and propel us to progress.

Some of my most enduring memories from college— from 1969 to 1974 at the University of Oregon in Eugene— lead me to this conclusion, and it's no surprise. I always have been more of a night owl than an early bird. Still, there is no question that, in the years after high school, when we are living away from home and seeking tangible keys to the future, we are more likely than ever to push boundaries in the quest for meaning.

For me, this sometimes emerged in a harmless act of boldness, such as riding my bicycle the wrong way on an empty 13th Avenue, swerving, skidding, and creating spiral street patterns illumined only by streetlights during a rare midnight snowfall. Or joining friends on a different snowy night to walk through the downtown mall and toss mushy snowballs that left faint, icy impressions on the large, square pattern adorning the walls of the upper floors of J.C. Penney, in an impromptu game of Tic-Tac-Toe. Or sauntering with a roommate over a no-pedestrians-allowed freeway bridge to Valley River Twin Cinemas several nights in a row to absorb the artistry and emotion of the reissued *Midnight Cowboy*, the Oscar-winning ode to unlikely friendship.

It's fair to say that most of my lasting college memories underscore the value of human relationships. Several such experiences draw from my chosen course of study, journalism, from its application in my work on the student newspaper, the *Oregon Daily Emerald*, and from the tumultuous tenor of the times.

In my fledgling *Emerald* reporting days in mid-November 1969, I accepted an assignment that, as I recall, no one else wanted. It was to cover an all-night vigil in the city park blocks, following a more prominent daytime anti–Vietnam War march of more than 2,500 people as part of the nationwide Moratorium. To gather enough information to write about the vigil, I could have stayed for an hour or two and left, but I was determined to remain present and awake and to take notes through the bitter cold of the wee hours till dawn. This let me report the ebb and flow of the crowd that thinned to fifty hardy souls and their mostly friendly encounters with police and other visitors. An insignificant story, perhaps, and it ran on an inside page, but today I reflect on it as a genuine attempt to encounter and reveal a slice of humanity.

A year later, as anti-war fervor intensified, and I moved into covering the administration beat, I worked many nights writing stories for the next morning's editions, and in October 1970, a late-night bomb blast at the university's tallest academic building found me already poised in the third-floor *Emerald* office to contribute to the coverage. My most vivid memory in those overnight hours, however, is not of gathering the news, but of standing on the windowsill, staring into the darkness, and engaging in quiet conversation with the woman who, a dozen years later, became my wife.

The following May, after 10:00 on a Thursday night during a protest near the ROTC building on Alder Street next to the campus, I was assigned to relieve a reporter who had to return to the office to write the deadline story that would appear in the Friday morning paper. When I got to the scene, hundreds of young demonstrators remained in a standoff with a formidable squad of county sheriff reservists, and the groups repeatedly surged tentatively at each other and backed off. Finally, the officers charged the crowd, and in the melee, several officers ran to the top of a nearby grassy bank where I was taking notes, and one of them beat me to the ground. I tried to say that I could show him my press card, but holding his club in my back, he was in no mood to talk.

Soon I was herded with scores of protesters to the city jail, where we talked through the night. Near dawn, thanks to the intervention of our editor and the university president, the city police chief released me, and I later wrote a story about the experience for the front page of the Monday morning edition. What I recall most from the ordeal, though, was the heartwarming evidence I discovered of the bond that I shared with fellow *Emerald* staffers. Departing the jail as the sun began to rise, I walked about ten blocks back to the newspaper office, where on the blackboard someone had scrawled in giant letters "FREE CLAY!"

Two years later, in spring 1973, after innumerable hours of hard work in nearly every role on the paper, I mounted an exhaustive campaign to be selected as editor for the coming academic year, and in the weeks leading to the culminating interview by the governing board, everything seemed aligned for my success. To my shock, however, during the interview I was asked an inflammatory question that accused me of something wholly inaccurate, and instantly I felt crushed. I stumbled through a reply, but it didn't matter. The damage was done, and there was no way for my candidacy to stay viable. Leaving the interview, I felt as outraged as I have ever been, but I somehow stuffed my distress and returned to the newspaper office to conduct an already-scheduled interview of two students who were running for student body president and vice president. As quickly as I could, I typed up the story and turned it in for the next day's paper. In a downcast daze, I walked slowly in the dark toward my apartment along a hushed 13th Avenue—and there, walking toward me, was my girlfriend. Unbidden, she had come to console me.

Over the years, these and other experiences gave me a simple but profound philosophy, which is that no matter what any of us believes about how or why we all got here, we are not meant to be hermits on this earth, hiding from the rest of the world. Rather, we are meant to connect with and inspire each other. Appropriately enough, as I grew older, I ended up writing books on two entertainers who embraced that way of thinking, and I emulate it every day.

Yes, life is all about love, respect, trust, compassion, and other core ideals, but none of it happens without present-moment, look-each-other-in-the-eye, breathe-the-same-air human relationships. And much of the time, unwittingly, we learn this at night.

Long before Dr. Scott Berkenblit became a surgeon, he was a freshman at MIT. He shares his recollection of an unusual and somewhat controversial college tradition, the Baker House Piano Drop:

While the Massachusetts Institute of Technology is probably best known for its prowess in education and research, the Institute is also home to a variety of quirky and distinctive traditions. Certainly one of the quirkiest is the Baker House Piano Drop.

One of a group of MIT dormitories, Baker House, was designed by Finnish architect Alvar Aalto and features striking views of the Boston skyline across the Charles River. Within its brick walls reside approximately 300 undergraduate students, who, as different generations of the MIT community, try to develop elegant and novel solutions to challenging technical problems.

Just such a challenge arose when the dorm found itself with an old dilapidated piano on its hands that was deemed to be unsalvageable. At a house meeting, a Baker resident named Charlie Bruno suggested it would probably be easier to get rid of a pile of piano pieces than to dispose of an intact piano. The problem, therefore, was to determine an effective and efficient way to reduce said piano to its constituent parts. A quick review of the MIT student handbook confirmed that, while students were prohibited from throwing objects out of dormitory windows, there was no rule that explicitly prohibited dropping objects off the roof of the buildings.

Amid much fanfare, the piano was brought up to the roof of Baker House and dropped over the side onto Amherst Alley, the street behind the building. While the resulting hole in the pavement was quickly repaired and forgotten, an enduring MIT tradition had been created.

By the time I arrived at MIT, the Piano Drop had become a venerated Baker House tradition, at least whenever an appropriate piano could be obtained. On the day of the event, a large crowd of Baker residents gathered on Amherst Alley, standing well back from the large "X" on the pavement that marked the impact zone.

After a few false starts (to tease the crowd), the crew on the roof launched the piano down a short ramp and over the edge. Following a few seconds of free fall, the piano slammed into the ground with a loud and surprisingly sonorous clang.

The spectators immediately rushed in to search the resulting pile of rubble for souvenirs. I ended up with one of the coveted pedals, which I used as a paperweight for the next 4 years, as well as a black piano key, which turned out to be the perfect size to replace the missing handle on our dorm room refrigerator.

Beyond the physical mementos, however, I gained from the event a satisfying sense of having helped, if only in a small way, to celebrate and perpetuate a timeless and unique MIT tradition.

Attorney Matthew Weissman, a graduate of Brown University, writes about how his work-study opportunities contributed to a productive college experience that continues to influence him to this day:

I showed up at college with no understanding of how it was all supposed to work into a career (unless you were pre-med), but I did know that I needed a job when I showed up in Providence. Ever since I was 12 years old, I had survived by working any kind of job. This included babysitting on Saturday nights and delivering newspapers in the summer and in the winter (one particular day I still remember delivering 30-40 *Daily News* papers on a 12-degree dark morning). And on to an office delivery job in New York City, a classic deli, an aquarium/pet shop, and then to Flushing Meadows Park. Every manner of fun, disgusting job, I had it.

So when I showed up at the work-study office early on the very first morning of Freshman Week at Brown, I got handed an unbelievably plum job—cashier at a late-night burger/chili joint. No working behind the counter, no dealing with the pots and pans. And, to top it all off, the cashier was in charge of the music.

Every Monday night through both freshman semesters and beyond, I was the man at the East Campus Dining Center. It got me away from the library and the dorm for one weeknight. I met and hung out with lots of impressive upperclassmen, made some lifelong friends, and just worked my way more broadly into life at my new school.

Other opportunities to work on campus arose over time. I grabbed many of them, from academic (computer programming in the geophysics lab) to arty (I did set construction and ran an auxiliary sound board for amazing Gospel productions by a professional theater company that was resident on campus), all for the standard, slightly-above-minimum-wage work-study pay.

This work kept me grounded and fed. It became part of the whole college experience for me, maybe as much as the classes, assignments, and overall academic challenges. College would not have been nearly as rich, or productive, without these opportunities.

A Teacher or Mentor Who Changed My Life

Eddy Friedfeld is a New York-based attorney and writer. He is also an adjunct professor at New York University and a visiting lecturer at Yale University. Eddy explains how he came to appreciate how faculty members can both challenge and support their students:

When a professor goes out of his way to challenge and support you, take it. It will always take you to a better place.

When I was a senior at Columbia University with aspirations of becoming a writer, I took a course called "The Author and Publisher" that was taught by Sam Vaughan, a veteran editor who had become the head of Doubleday and Company, and who worked with writers as diverse as President Dwight D. Eisenhower, William F. Buckley Jr., Bruce Catton, and Fannie Flagg.

Sam was knowledgeable and interesting, but equally important, he was passionate, enthusiastic, and approachable. He worked with many celebrities, but made the students feel that we were the highlight of his week. I remember little about what he said and every detail about how he inspired my classmates and me. I wrote an essay for him with as much passion as I ever wrote anything before and he responded with commensurate enthusiasm.

At the end of the last class, he said, "If I can help you in any way, please call."

Every year was the year I was going to start writing professionally. One year, I bought Larry Gelbart's autobiography. Larry, who through an almost 70-year career moved deftly and effortlessly between Broadway, film, and television, had started his career in radio writing for

Danny Thomas and Bob Hope, then in television for Sid Caesar. He scripted *Tootsie*, *A Funny Thing Happened on the Way to the Forum*, *Mastergate*, and is most famous for creating the television version of *M*A*S*H*, one of my favorite shows as a kid, and now as an adult. For my friends and me, Larry made it hip to be smart, driven, and charitable. I noticed in the acknowledgments that the book was edited by Sam Vaughan. I took it as an omen. Within a month I was writing movie reviews and feature pieces for *The North Carolina Daily Record*, whom I still proudly write for today, 16 years later. That led me to pieces in the *New York Post*, the *New York Times*, and the *Daily News*, as well as interviews that included Francis Ford Coppola, Mel Brooks, Carl Reiner, Billy Crystal, Eric Idle, Whoopi Goldberg, and Sid Caesar, whose autobiography I co-wrote.

I could picture the look on Sam's assistant's face when I called and said: "He said, if you need anything, call. I know it's been 18 years, but here I am."

I knew it was an unusual call, but I knew Sam well enough to know that he would enjoy hearing from me and be eager to help. He could not have been more helpful. I sent him my writing. He gave me insight and guidance, and, once again, inspiration.

Sid Caesar led me to Larry Gelbart, with whom I developed a great friendship until his passing. He was one of the great wits of the 20th century and probably any other century.

When I began teaching college 10 years ago, I thought of Sam, as well as other great professors I had, both in the preparation of the courses and in my approach to students.

Almost every week, I hear from at least one former student seeking advice or an opinion, or simply wanting to share something they watched or read that reminded them of my class and me. I think of Sam and feel like I'm paying it forward.

Even if you are full of creative fuel, you need someone to ignite the spark that propels you and to guide you. Sam was one of those special and inspirational people, and I've tried to be the same person for every student I have taught and will teach.

Tad Daley, author of the book Apocalypse Never: Forging the Path to a Nuclear Weapon-Free World, *shares what happened to him after he got a C+ on his first college paper:*

I got a C+ on the first paper I ever wrote in college. The class was Political Science 101, at Knox College in Galesburg, Illinois, and the professor was one Philip S. Haring. He had us all read *The Republic*, written by one Plato, and he invited us all to write him a short essay telling us what we thought of it.

In my paper, I informed Professor Haring that I had come to the definitive conclusion that Plato's book was "no good." Why? Because, I had brilliantly discovered, it was "just too unrealistic." I then proceeded to provide Professor Haring with numerous examples of just what kind of history had happened in "the real world"—demonstrating just how closely I had paid attention in my world history class at John Hersey High School in Arlington Heights, Illinois—contrasting it with what I declared could only be called Plato's "dream world."

He returned the paper to me with no comments at all, other than that big red "C+" at the top.

I stormed up to his office and pounded on the door.

"Come in."

Plato's *Republic* was unrealistic, I announced. "Just look at the records of the ages," I insisted. "Plus," I informed him, "I have been told many times that I am a really good writer." Had the Knox admissions office failed to inform him that I had sent them some of the articles I had written for the Hersey school newspaper, *The Correspondent*, along with my application?

Professor Haring listened to me quite patiently. Perplexingly, he didn't seem to disagree with any of the points I repeatedly made. But, finally, in precisely the fashion, I later realized, of one Socrates, he began to ask me some questions.

"Do you think, Mr. Daley, that it is just possible that Plato, whose works, after all, have endured for some reason for a good 25 centuries, might have been almost as smart as a bright young man such as yourself?"

"Well, I suppose…"

"And do you think, Mr. Daley, that it is just possible that Plato, although not having access, of course, to the subsequent 25 centuries of history available to you, might have known something about the various forms of political organization, the fundamentals of human nature, and the record of the previous 25 centuries or so since the dawn of human civilization?"

"Well, I guess…"

"And do you think, Mr. Daley, that it is just possible that Plato himself might have recognized that the polity he described in *The Republic* was, as you say, "unrealistic," and unlikely ever to be attained in, as you say, "the real world?"

"Well, I never really thought about that…"

"So why do you suppose then, Mr. Daley, that Plato might have invented a vision of what he considered to be an ideal human society if he knew full well that such an ideal almost certainly would never be reached?"

"Hmmmm…"

"Why don't you get lost now?"

I spent many hours in Knox's Seymour Library contemplating our conversation. And, eventually, I got it through my thick skull that in any kind of human endeavor, one had to have a goal. An aspiration. A destination. Yes, a journey of a thousand miles might begin with a single step—

but you have to know which way to go, whether to set out east or west, what you are journeying toward. We tread mile after arduous mile on the pathway to the mountaintop—even if we cannot see it because it is perpetually shrouded in clouds—because we have some dream of what we might find at the summit.

In addition, said Robert Browning, "A man's reach should exceed his grasp, or what's a heaven for?" Even if we don't ever reach our goals, ever live our dreams, ever achieve peace on Earth and goodwill toward women and men and 999 other far-distant hoped-for destinies, perhaps by articulating our dreams, we might at least get a little bit closer to realizing them.

John Hersey (for whom my high school was named) had sort of done the opposite, bringing us face to face not with our highest ideals but our descent into darkness, when he described for the readers of *The New Yorker* magazine in the autumn of 1945 the unprecedented and incomprehensible devastation wrought by the atomic bombing of the city of Hiroshima. And Plato himself, among many other singularities, by any reckoning stands in the pantheon of history as humanity's first feminist. A long 2,500 years later, gender equality is parsecs away in much of the world, and has yet to be fully attained anywhere in the world. But we're a lot closer than we were 2,500 years ago, perhaps, one might posit, in small part, because Plato first charted the course.

I got better grades on most of the subsequent papers I wrote in college. And a few decades later, when I finally got around to writing my first book, about the dream of someday dismantling every last nuclear weapon on the face of the Earth and inventing new global governance architectures to ensure that they will never return to haunt the human condition again, I dedicated it to no less than seven people.

My late parents, Diana J. Daley and Claude Daley Jr.

My beloved wife, Kitty Felde.

And for H. G. Wells, George F. Kennan, Robert A. Heinlein, and Professor Philip S. Haring of Knox College, who taught me to ponder not only what we are, but what we might become.

Dr. Ed Gomes is Director of Spiritual Development for the Liberty University football team and is on the pastoral staff at Thomas Road Baptist Church in Lynchburg, Virginia. He is a Liberty graduate himself. One of eleven children, Ed was offered a Liberty basketball scholarship and was then a starting point guard for the Liberty Flames for three years. He shares a life-changing experience from his college days:

I can vividly remember sitting down with my head basketball coach, getting ready to tell him that I had decided to leave what was then called Lynchburg Baptist College and had now become Liberty University.

I wanted to talk to my coach about something serious that had been on my mind for a while. That question was, "Is it possible to be a Christian and be prejudiced?"

After giving some serious thought to the question, I concluded that, while it was wrong, it was possible to be a Christian and be prejudiced.

In no way did I hear or experience any kind of prejudice from the administration or faculty or student body.

In fact, I remember talking with Dr. Jerry Falwell about the matter, and he said to me, "Ed, my door is always open. Be patient and in time things will change." Yes, it has changed, and the cloud of doubt has been removed. Praise the Lord.

As I look back over the experience, it was about the beginning of a change that was not only taking place at Liberty University, but a transformation that was also taking place at colleges around the country. Blacks and whites were beginning to integrate from all walks of life.

My life-changing experience had to do with accepting the wisdom, insight, and practical advice that I received from my head coach to stay in school. He told me, "Do not let that kind of conclusion about life keep you from a life-changing opportunity through receiving a college education."

Taking his advice has taught me to help others appreciate the advice one receives when having difficulty dealing with everyday issues. Even to this day, I still consider that moment to be a life-changing experience. To God be the glory.

Cathleen Hanson, a graduate of Towson University and now director of the International School of Protocol, recounts a comment by her Speech 100 teacher that changed the direction of her life. Notice that Cathleen's follow-through also contributed to her success:

I was sixteen when I started college. My plan was to go to the college where my father was a math professor and then transfer after a year. I planned on completing college in two and a half years and then going to law school.

None of this happened, because in my first semester at college I took a general education class that filled an available time slot. It was Speech 100. I never considered myself a good speaker, and I had tons of stage fright. On top of that, I had performance anxiety and problems with procrastination (not good for public speaking that has multiple steps and that includes research, writing, and practice).

Nonetheless, when I gave my first speech on backpacking, it was interesting or entertaining enough for the teacher to ask if I had any interest in joining the Speech and Debate Team. At that point, I was living at home, and the thought of traveling around the country on weekends for speech and debate competitions was very appealing. I had a sense of adventure—hence the backpacking. So, I joined the team, and it was undoubtedly the best academic experience imaginable.

I didn't transfer. I stayed at the same college for four years with a new objective: to be a top competitive speaker. I won some national championships, which helped get me into a highly selective graduate program in the field of Communication Theory and Research.

After completing my graduate coursework, my sense of adventure took me to Alaska in the domestic Peace Corps. Afterward, I took a teaching job at the University of Alaska. I quickly formed the first-ever speech and debate team for the university, which in turn attracted all kinds of attention because our fledgling team came back from California and the Pacific Northwest with big trophies and lots of first place awards.

We were featured in the paper and on television. We were big news for a relatively small town. One of the Alaska state legislators who had been on a speech and debate team as an undergraduate recognized the value of the program. At that point, our team received unprecedented line item funding from the State of Alaska.

Jennifer K., Boston University Class of 1993, had this to share about a professor who encouraged her to do extra work above and beyond her required classwork:

In my first year of college, I chose a number of new classes to test my interests, including Geology. I thought it would be a fun course, not unlike how the uninitiated think of Astronomy. I carried a full load and was doing well in all my courses, except for Geology. I was always a good student, so this came as a shock, and it began weighing heavily on my mind as well as affecting my GPA. I decided to talk to the professor to ask if he would consider any extra credit work for the class. I was sure he would turn me down,

110

especially because he had been sticking firmly to the syllabus. To my great surprise, he agreed, and suggested an extra credit paper on any rocks of my choosing. My deadline was at the end of the coming break. I had recently been to Lanzarote Island, which was created by ancient volcanic eruptions, leaving a moonscape with extravagant rock formations. Perfect.

I learned a few things. First, always try to experience something new. Second, do not panic when you discover that something might be outside of your comfort zone. Then try to formulate a plan to achieve the best outcome, even if your plan was not on the original syllabus or business plan. Finally, don't feel guilty if you don't master every subject. Not everyone should be a geologist.

Actress and model Kristina Korsholm reflects on her studies at UCLA in 2000, especially her work with her directing professor. A native of Denmark, Kristina is a graduate of Stockholm University and the University of Copenhagen:

I took acting and directing at UCLA. My directing professor, Michael McLain, was a very cool and inspiring teacher who took the time to listen and help even the goofiest outsiders (me included). He pulled me aside one day, and we discussed how I could communicate the scene I was planning to direct to my actors in the best possible way.

I was working on a scene by the famous Spanish poet and playwright Federico García Lorca. Instead of giving me the usual analysis of Lorca's texts, Michael blew my mind by emphasizing connections between art and society, and then introducing me to Spanish art and history at the time of the play, particularly to works by Joan Miró.

My homework was to visit museums to see paintings that would inspire me and give me a deeper understanding of Lorca's voice. I found myself mesmerized by a newfound understanding of how art can also be a political voice. It's not like I hadn't thought about that before and understood it on an intellectual level, but this time, I really felt it under my skin.

Arts, politics, and science are all connected. So are music, film, theater, and literature. New inventions within science create new opportunities for society, and these new opportunities inspire the mood and environment of our great artists and filmmakers, which, in turn, is reflected in their work.

Studying made a lot of sense to me when I got around to this understanding. I developed the appetite to learn how things are united and to understand the greater meaning of why things happen and how we are part of it all.

Fifteen years after my UCLA experience, I was in Zurich at the Kunsthaus where Miró was showing. I was there with my mother-in-law and I found myself speaking with her about the influence of politics on Spanish artists, music, and plays. I was quite surprised how I had stored all that knowledge. But it was there. And I know it was because a professor at UCLA took the time to work with me in 2000.

Katherine Dayton, a 1996 graduate of Dickinson College, shares how she moved from wanting a job to wanting to change the world:

My academic interests during college revolved around environmental studies. That is where I focused most of my course load, my friendships, and my passion. Environmental studies was then only a certificate program at Dickinson, not yet a degree program, so I had to choose a major. I chose policy studies, which felt generic enough that it could complement my interests in conservation issues. Also, it was the only degree that required being accepted through a separate application process, which appealed to me.

For the first couple of years, I didn't seem to fit in socially with my cohorts. I was the only student in my graduating class from Montana and one of the few from the West. While being from a Rocky Mountain state may not seem like a significant gap, when I look back on my college years, where most of the student body was from the East Coast, there were distinct cultural differences. I remember my basketball teammates saying that they liked the slow cadence of speech of Montanans (I was the only Montanan any of them knew at the time). I also didn't share a lot of the reference points: boarding school life, seaboard vacations, etc.

It's hard to place a finger on culture shock when people look like you, but I was probably more out of my element than I've been during dozens of subsequent life experiences in Latin America, Southeast Asia, Ghana, and various Caribbean countries.

So while the environmental studies program is where I found my "tribe," I enjoyed the contrasts and complements of the policy work. It wasn't until my senior seminar, though, that it all came together. A professor, Mara Donaldson, made what felt like a bold statement, and she was passionate about it. "Here is the thing," she said during a lecture, "all of you want a job, but I want you to change the world." I was dumbstruck for a moment. It's the single line from any Dickinson class that I can remember verbatim to this day. She put words to a sentiment I'd had, but that I couldn't put a finger on yet. She made me think about possibilities that were more ambiguous and challenging, compared to what felt like the simple task of just finding a job.

I often return to Professor Donaldson's appeal as a check-in with myself, and the hopes for what my life would be from that senior seminar moment.

I've come to realize that, on a day-by-day basis, I am not always changing the world in significant ways. However, I am having a positive impact. I now own and direct an organization that runs international community service programs. We take teenagers, mostly from the United States, to locations in under-resourced communities around the world. There they work as volunteers doing construction projects and other hands-on initiatives. While much of my work is now administrative, there is a ripple effect from the tasks that my colleagues and I do every day.

In the end, what I really want is to be busy working on projects that in some way tie in with a bigger meaning and contribute to positive change for the world. I am happy my work aligns with my values. I derive satisfaction from doing things well, taking ownership, and realizing that each piece fits in to the larger work and meaning that comes from the international volunteer programs we run.

Tiffany Harris is a Country Desk Officer at the Peace Corps. She explains how her college, Seattle University, ruined her for good:

Weighing all the schools that had accepted me, I decided to attend Seattle University, where I would be taught by Jesuit priests and go to mass as part of the curriculum. Even though the school was focused on the Jesuit mission and identity, which included a commitment to the poor and to issues of social responsibility, I was mainly attracted to the fixed-gear bikes and all the hipsters I saw on campus.

I entered college ambitious, driven, and fixated on the idea of making a lot of money once I graduated. I figured that majoring in business and finance was a good start.

I don't remember even signing up for it, but I ended up in an academic program called "The Faith and the Great Ideas Learning Community." The idea behind this community was to help students become more aware of the foundations of their own beliefs and values, and to confront the structures that perpetuate poverty and injustice. During my first semester, I had two professors, Dr. Michael

114

Matriotti and Dr. Mary-Antoinette Smith, who became my mentors that year.

One of my courses dealt with the causes and consequences of poverty in America. We read texts and engaged in conversations that surrounded philosophy, environmentalism, and economics. We read a book called *Small Is Beautiful,* which focused on "people-centered economics." Dr. Smith taught me about cultural pluralism and personal spirituality.

Four years later, I graduated with a degree in communication studies and business administration, and, just like I planned, I signed a contract, large bonus included, to be a clothing buyer with a nationwide department store. It was supposed to be my dream job.

But my dream job came with a lot of ethical dilemmas. From manufacturing practices abroad, to daily fulfillment, I struggled. I thought a lot about everything I had learned in college, and I tried to connect my job, the thing I was doing for 8 hours a day, 5 days a week, to social justice and to the greater community that I had spent so much time considering.

After one of the factories from which we sourced clothing joined a labor union, we dropped them. I remember seeing some of my college friends among union and anti-sweatshop activists protesting outside my office building.

I made a difficult, but conscious decision, and I sent a resignation email to my supervisor that afternoon.

I took my signing bonus and travelled around the world. I joined the Peace Corps, went to graduate school, learned three new languages, and found a meaningful career.

My college experience was a life-changing journey. I like to say that Seattle University ruined me for good because my professors and mentors challenged and prepared me for a life of purpose.

Some aspects of my life have become more challenging because I work in international development, but I feel good about the impact my work is having. I've been able to integrate spirituality and justice, I have a strong sense of community, and I have grown to become a better and more fulfilled person.

Bruce Dehnert is head of ceramics at Peters Valley School of Craft in New Jersey. He recounts his path from creative writing to ceramics—via Hunter College and Alfred University:

If there's one thing that artists, regardless of their temperaments, can teach the world, it's their interest in and embrace of possibilities. The realm of "what is possible" is the lifeblood, the business acumen, of artists.

The challenge of deciding what to do in my life was connected to this concept of art, though I don't remember being aware of it at the time. There are people and strategies to help us better understand what our aptitudes are, but each of us has, on an unconscious level, a deep knowledge of what makes us tick. The trick is to get in there, be honest with ourselves, and then make choices for that particular time in our lives.

In 1986, I was working in my small pottery studio at the foot of the Wind River Mountains in Wyoming. It was December and there was deep snow outside. The phone rang, and on the other end of the line was Susan Peterson, former head of the ceramics department at the University of Southern California.

She invited me to come to New York City to teach a semester-long class in pottery because one of her colleagues at Hunter College, where Susan then taught, had suddenly announced plans to take a leave of absence. My curiosity about a big city far away on the East Coast and my embrace of possibilities guided my answer to Susan's invitation. It set me on my eventual journey to Alfred University and eventually to New Zealand and the island of Borneo.

When I first moved to New York, I assumed it would be for only a few months. Wanting to make the most of my time there, I became almost fanatical about visiting museums, seeing plays, listening to the wide array of music the city had to offer, and basically opening up to experiences I couldn't have in Wyoming.

I had gone to school previously for creative writing and my "lens" was focused primarily on the people of New York. Viewing them as characters in short stories, poems, and novels, I noticed that New Yorkers were different from Wyomingites. One day, there was the Italian taxi driver explaining Plato's disdain for artists, and the next day, on the 7 train, I was listening to a talkative high school student on his way to Queens. These new experiences were captivating, and I began to try to represent these "characters" in my art. But doing this required that I consider the possibility of using sculpture, rather than pottery, to describe the fantastical scenes playing out on and under the city's streets.

I knew practically nothing about sculpture. After a few years in New York, and lots of sculptures later, I decided to go to school to undertake a more serious study of the discipline. But I didn't quite know how to do that, and this is where my mentor came in.

Susan was a force of nature. She had built ceramic programs on both coasts, written numerous books on ceramics, and was a fervent believer in young artists forging paths according to their aspirations. She was an articulate, strong woman who had navigated a life of teaching and making art in a man's world, and she was resolute in making sure that the young people around her had a dynamic example to follow. Knowing this, I asked for her advice on the quandary of which school to apply to, and in typical fashion, she in turn followed with a question:

"Whose work and ideas do you admire most?" she asked.

When I reminded her that I didn't have an art background, I remember her answering, "During your interview, I'm sure you'll convince them that if it doesn't matter to you, why should it matter to them?"

With that, I set about searching for a sculptor whose work I admired, ignoring the roadblocks I had set for myself.

Finding my answer was a matter of reading articles written by artists, and delving into journals, magazines, and books. I looked for photographs of sculptures that excited me and I tried to understand why. One artist whose work I kept coming back to was Tony Hepburn. Born in England, Hepburn had been a member of a group of conceptual artists who labeled themselves the "Art and Language Movement." They tended to be a surly bunch of British artists who believed it was possible that art could be distilled to nearly nothingness. They argued that meaning is found not in objects but in the language around those objects.

The Art and Language Movement attracted a great deal of attention in the international art world, and it wasn't long before Hepburn packed his bags and made his way to the United States, where conceptual art was in full swing. Upon moving to New York, his sculptures began to resemble workers' and farmers' tools, clothing, and implements. These facsimiles stood as symbols for the people who used the tools and for the hardscrabble lives they led, but whose depictions were generally absent from sculptures and installations. The work was full of vitality and a sense of the handmade. My own interests were in portraying the characters, so Hepburn's work piqued my interest in the contradiction.

I learned that Hepburn was teaching at Alfred University, a highly regarded college in rural New York State. So I applied.

To my surprise, I was granted an interview. Remembering Susan's advice, I nervously sat down in a small office across the desk from Professor Hepburn.

Sure enough, the first question he asked was, "What makes you think you should be admitted without a degree in art?"

I answered, "Because it isn't my intention to make sculptures that tell stories about the world in which art degrees are an essential part."

He looked straight at me over his reading glasses and, without smiling, said, "That's one of the craziest answers I've ever heard in one of these interviews."

I began my studies at Alfred in 1989.

In the early months of my time at Alfred, my work loosely resembled Hepburn's. His influence through work and ideas were a powerful draw for me, and I struggled with finding a way to locate my own "voice." Under the glaring spotlight that is trained on Alfred's ceramics students, there were many times I seriously doubted my ability to distinguish that voice. But somewhere along the line, after I'd failed a couple of semesters, and during one of our weekly conversations, Professor Hepburn challenged me to explain my use of memory as a conceptual element in my work.

As Hepburn left my studio that afternoon, I noticed the emptiness of its walls. Although I had hung a few drawings and photos near one corner, mostly there was vacant space extending all the way around the periphery of the room. When I walked over to my worktable, I was surprised to find a Sharpie marker resting on top of a small pile of dried clay. Ignoring whether or not finding the pen was a strange sign, I immediately went searching for a ladder in the maintenance department.

Returning to my studio with a candy-orange stepladder, I positioned it in the corner farthest from the door. In the uppermost reaches of one of the four walls, in the same corner one would begin writing on a piece of paper, I began to write my memories. Over the next year and a half, I filled the walls from their top edges to the floor. I wrote anything that came to mind having to do with memory, relationships, and observations of the world. I kept my letters no taller than two inches, and because I didn't use straight lines, the visual form of the writing took a natural wave-like shape.

After a semester, with the walls becoming more and more filled with a maze of sentences, I began to recognize connections between many of my thoughts. As ideas and relationships fraught with complexity emerged, I responded by building life-scale sculptures with some of the characters present in the writing. I placed segmented figures in various positions, separated by walls, giving a distinct association with architecture, obstacle, and disconnection. Because I was finally able to relate writing and memory to my sculpture, I became more aware of various realities of my own life. And because I was at a school where experimentation and exploration were considered paramount, I had begun to find that always-elusive "voice."

Since those days at Alfred, I have continued to explore many of the same forms, with each new body of work providing greater opportunity to hone my viewpoints and reflections. After retiring from a long career at Hunter College, Susan wrote a few more books, and sadly passed away several years ago. I learned from her that with persistence I could achieve goals that otherwise seemed out of reach. From Tony Hepburn, who also recently passed away, I learned to trust my own voice and to build only the walls I need, not the ones that stand in my way.

Food and nutrition scientist Dr. Joy Dubost shares how a conversation with her Hood College nutrition professor led her from healthy cookies to a Ph.D. in Food Science:

I was in my junior year at Hood College and had recently declared nutrition as a major. One of my courses required that I develop a healthier recipe for chocolate chip cookies, which would be lower in calories and fat but still delicious.

At the time, I had declared chemistry as a minor. Applying what I learned in Chemistry 101 and Organic Chemistry, I realized I could make the cookies even better by applying some basic chemistry principles, including analytical analysis. With this, I approached my nutrition professor and asked if I could take the project a step further and include chemical analysis that would ultimately affect the texture and flavor profile of the cookies.

Much to my delight, my nutrition professor was all on board, and even asked that I present my findings to the entire class. Yes, the cookies were delicious, and I received an A in the assignment.

At the time, I didn't realize it but I was creating my own "food science" major, which my college did not have. After this experience, I decided to declare chemistry as my second major, which actually extended my time in college by a full academic year. Moving forward, I integrated my chemistry and nutrition classes to ensure I was combining both scientific disciplines.

If I had never thought of integrating my majors or even applying principles of one scientific discipline into another scientific discipline, my career could have taken a much different direction. I ended up receiving a master's and Ph.D. in Food Science, but it all really started with a chocolate chip cookie.

Debra Polsky, Executive Director of the Dallas Jewish Historical Society, talks about how a college professor helped her develop self-confidence and opened her mind to multiple opportunities:

Prior to entering my freshman year at Southwestern at Memphis (now Rhodes College), I was certain I would have a career as an attorney. My mother had been a legal secretary my entire life and her boss was a strong male figure in my life, as my father had died when I was a young child. Financing college was a challenge, so I took the opportunity

121

to spend the summer on campus at a work-study position and was assigned to the international studies department, working for Dr. David Likes.

Known as "The Colonel," Dr. Likes had been an important career Army officer. He took a liking to me and convinced me that I should take his international studies class in the fall. I did, and continued to work in the international studies department. Dr. Likes was a brilliant teacher, although tough, and his own experiences with the Army, NATO, and other assignments made the world and politics come to life.

Although I had always loved history, learning from the Colonel in a small class setting exposed me to more than dates and places. We studied American history from a diplomatic point of view—not just what happened, but also the context and personalities involved. Additionally, I was exposed to people on the ground. Friends of the Colonel would visit, speak, dine, and interact with the twelve students in the class. These included the sitting British Ambassador and the Czechoslovakian Ambassador to the United Nations. For the first time, history became a living, breathing entity that affected my life and the lives of others.

Most important for me, though, was the encouragement I received. I knew I was smart, had always been a good student, but lacked self-confidence. Dr. Likes encouraged me to open my mind to the vast possibilities in the world. He encouraged me to study Arabic; to take classes on the Vietnam conflict (still going on at the time) and on the history of the United Nations (and to participate in college-level model U.N. gatherings); and to consider a career in government and diplomacy.

While his vision for me as the first female ambassador to Egypt was not ultimately my vision, his belief in me did give me the courage to really think about what I could do and where I wanted to do it. Would my life have been different as an attorney? Certainly, but my engagement with

122

a master teacher ultimately led me to discover my own ability to help others see the past and the future as a continuum.

Violist, violinist, and singer Kiara Ana Perico is a 2011 graduate of Boston University's music school. She was part of the "Glee Band" for Season Six of "Glee" and has toured with the Trans-Siberian Orchestra, Adele, Bleu, and Ariana Grande. She shares how her viola professor taught her much more than the mechanics of playing the viola:

I graduated high school next to a field of cows in Western Massachusetts, surrounded by seven of the strongest girls I've ever encountered. I didn't go to an all-girls school, but there just weren't any boys in our class. I went on to the Boston University School of Music to study viola performance with Professor Michelle LaCourse. Although I haven't pursued a career as an orchestral musician or college professor, my life was altered and influenced greatly by this incredible woman and by the way she approached viola and music education.

Needless to say, it was a bit of a culture shock moving from an incredibly small town to the big city and from outdoor classrooms into huge lecture halls. I felt like a really small fish in the biggest ocean. But my weekly time with Professor LaCourse moved me past the sheer number of people swirling around me at the university, and helped me form how I was going to navigate the rest of my life, with and without my instrument. She incorporated ancient body and mind movement and intention into our lessons. This, in turn, inspired me to cultivate a totally different relationship with my body, the way I moved, both physically and emotionally, and the people I surrounded myself with.

Now, whether I'm sound-checking at a concert hall in Berlin, Germany, playing an arena show at Madison Square Garden with fire exploding all around me, practicing yoga, or having a meaningful conversation with a friend, my actions are rooted in intention and love. My energy is drawn from a place deep within myself. Unexpectedly, but so thankfully, I started the journey of creating my adult self through my time with my viola professor in college.

College advisors, teachers, and mentors can have a profound impact on the lives of their students in all sorts of ways.

Bruce Payne, Distinguished Lecturer in Communication Studies at Baruch College, and former winner of Duke University's Undergraduate Teaching Award, clearly understands the impact of taking the time to get to know his students. He shares his eulogy of his former teacher at the University of California, Berkeley, Wilson Carey McWilliams:

In 1961, Carey lived on Walnut Street in Berkeley. Several of us had moved in nearby—Bill, Jerry, and Kate downstairs, John and I next door—and eight or ten others dropped by often. The more-or-less nightly living room seminar had hardly begun one evening when a freshman friend of mine came in for help with the Nietzsche he was required to read.

"Begin anywhere that looks promising," Carey said. "Don't go on to the next sentence until you've understood the first, and don't worry if that takes all night."

Around eleven, Bill came back to talk with Carey, still working on his first sentence. By dawn, as I remember, he'd gotten through a paragraph.

That spring, Carey had to choose: the job at Oberlin, or executive officer of the Airborne's Ready Division.

"You're a teacher," I urged on Oberlin's behalf. "What else would you be doing in the Army? But doesn't it matter what you teach?"

"Bruce," he laughed, "you know I always teach the same things."

That was unanswerably so. I had already learned from him, as from no other teacher before or since, how to read a sentence or a book—inquiringly, determinedly, ardently. And it was Carey who persuaded me that the best in the world was mine by right—indeed, that every one of us was fully entitled to Plato or Machiavelli, to Beethoven or Shakespeare, or Madison, or Robert Frost, or Rembrandt. What he taught was how to find ourselves, to know ourselves, to become who we might be—all that by means of passionately dialectical encounters with other minds, and more particularly with his.

For me, the great change began the afternoon I knocked on Carey's door for help with Plato. The visiting behavioralist had said in class that "the technique of the Platonic dialogue is to make everything explicit." Carey thought otherwise, as I knew from listening. But I had never gotten further than Socrates' words in the *Apology*.

Nevertheless, a sophomore, I challenged the professor: "Do you really believe that?" Now I wanted to make the case. "What should I read?"

Carey thought for a moment and took the *Protagoras* off the shelf—Plato's dialogue on how and whether virtue could be taught. He read three pages aloud—laughing! I had never guessed philosophy could be this funny. He gave me the thin paperback and told me to come back when I'd read it.

Returning in 2 hours, I was lost at sea. Carey, as usual, said to stay for dinner; afterward, he read a few more pages, stopping to look up the references to Homer. My second unsuccessful try took longer—6 hours. But the lights were still on next door, and the 2 a.m. recommendation was Aristophanes' comedy, *The Clouds*, as a kind of counterpoint. Fine advice still, especially for any terminally earnest and humor-impaired 19-year-old.

So it went. The sixth time, reading the book took a solid week. The long paper that ensued got a B. It was good, the behavioralist admitted, but very late. Carey found this so wrongheaded that over the summer he contrived with Norman Jacobson to register me in political science and put me in their honors program.

At my summer timber survey job in Northern California, I learned this only when Carey and a friend drove up on a Saturday in July, bringing my paper and some books for which I'd asked. On our way out to Redding from Harrison Gulch, the brakes failed in Carey's old Chevrolet, and he steered away from the cliff's edge into a nearby bank of earth: a soft landing for the three of us, though the car was totaled.

Waiting half an hour in the hot sun for the next car or truck, we talked about a favorite topic, the mysteries of desire. Carey held that eros was at least partly comic, citing the *Symposium*: Aristophanes' wondrous tale that humans were once happily spheroid, with four arms and four legs and various combinations of genitalia, but that Zeus had objected to their self-satisfaction, splitting each member of the race in two, and that everybody since has sought and sometimes even found that long-lost half.

Carey believed some mysteries can't be solved, but he held that myths and stories instead can often deepen them. And it is an abiding mystery that, for so many of us, he was and is our other half: our durable partner in dialogue, our permanently affectionate and unrelenting critic. I don't teach without his words in my mind, or make tough choices without asking: What would Socrates say now? Or Carey?

Or Mrs. Eleanor Roosevelt, for that matter, from whom Carey once learned something about politics he thought essential. At the 1952 Democratic Convention, Carey, 18 years old and an alternate delegate, was introduced in a receiving line.

"Oh, Carey McWilliams, I know your mother."

This was a relief from dozens of delegates who knew his activist father, and Carey was impressed that she had guessed that.

Nevertheless, she was the conscience of the Democratic Party, so honesty obliged: "Thank you, Mrs. Roosevelt, but I think you mean my stepmother, Iris McWilliams."

"Oh, no, I mean your mother, Dorothy McWilliams. She was chairman of the Al Smith campaign at UCLA in 1928, and she did a simply marvelous job."

Mrs. Roosevelt remembered. She did it all the time. Individuals mattered to her, as they did to Carey, mattered every bit as much as the principles for which she fought so hard.

Carey once wrote: "The community is primary; the ends are secondary, and derivative." I doubted this at first but was eventually persuaded. He meant, I think, that if we love each other generously, thoughtfully, and toughly enough, if we demand from each other the very best that we can be, then the ends, the values, the hopes we share and keep developing, are likely to be the right ones. They might even be deep enough or strong enough in time to reconstruct our fractured, fearful, still somehow democratic polity.

So, now, finally, Carey… We will remember you. How could we not? Nor will we lose your love for us, here, in our hearts, giving us such strength through all these many years.

Something I Couldn't Have Done Before

Charla Bailey, a graduate of Emporia State University and now Director of International Education at Texas Lutheran University, talks about her own study abroad experience and how she navigated her return to the United States:

I am originally from a small town in Kansas with a population of 1,000. Many of the people in my and my parents' circles of friends had never been outside of the United States, so it came as a shock to my mother when I announced that I wanted to go to Mexico. I had been invited to go to Puebla for five weeks as part of a study abroad program.

After discussing what I would be doing in Mexico, where I would be staying, and how I would be safe, my mother was supportive but still very worried about the whole experience. She grew up in a small town as well, and had never traveled abroad. Besides, I was her youngest child.

When I got to Mexico, I realized that it wasn't quite so different after all. The customs and personalities within the culture were new, but I was able to adapt pretty quickly. I participated in dances, group activities, and excursions from which I learned so much about the people of Puebla and their local traditions. Although I knew very little Spanish before going, I worked hard on my language skills. I had language teachers who were very patient and a host mother who assisted me as I studied Spanish grammar rules and practiced pronouncing difficult words. I used my newfound vocabulary in the market, on the bus, and with new friends.

Although it was great to see my mother upon my return to the United States, I had a difficult time readjusting to my former life. I found myself wanting to use the public bus and missing the times I went exploring with my Mexican friends. I remember asking myself why we need fifteen different kinds of ketchup and why we tend to rush so much. I longed for my daily life in Mexico with classes in the morning, lunch and a siesta, and then sightseeing in the afternoon with my language partner.

I also had some difficulty relating to my U.S. friends after I returned from Mexico. None of them had ever had the same type of experience. Some of them were excited to listen to my stories but others gave me about five minutes to share something about Mexico before moving on to other topics.

Over time, I ended up reestablishing close connections with my mother and my friends. However, I knew that I had changed. I became a lot more independent, and I wanted to keep my experiences abroad alive. At every opportunity, I spoke with community groups about my time in Mexico.

To this day, I continue to share the feelings I had both leading up to and following my studies in Puebla. Having taken the opportunity to learn abroad myself, I encourage and enthusiastically support my students as they prepare for their own study abroad experiences.

Washington consultant Dr. Mindy Reiser recounts her path from Brooklyn College to Oslo to the wider world:
The course on comedy and satire was illuminating; reading the letters of Cicero (all right, in English) was enlightening; and discovering the ancient Chinese court world described by historian Ssu-ma Ch'ien certainly opened cultural doors for me. But perhaps the exposure that mattered most had to do more with doing, with setting into motion, and with bringing something into being.

It was my Brooklyn College Alumni Fund Scholarship for Summer Study Abroad that propelled me from reading about other times and places to directly encountering another world—from Brooklyn, New York, to Norway and the University of Oslo. I lived in the Blindern Studenterhjem and learned about the sagas, Henrik Ibsen, the Arctic, and youth estrangement in an egalitarian society. We went on field trips, explored architecture and landscapes very different from Brooklyn, and were hosted at the Oslo City Hall. I sampled Nordic cuisine and I made my first acquaintance with Edvard Munch and his iconic *Scream*. My Scandinavian journey brought me into the world of St. Olaf College in Northfield, Minnesota—organizers over many years of the summer program at the University of Oslo. St. Olaf, a Lutheran institution, was a long way from my largely Jewish Brooklyn habitat—and an introduction to an American diversity I had never experienced.

And the journey did not end with my return to Brooklyn at summer's end. To take advantage of my newly acquired knowledge of at least one component of Scandinavian identity, I became the president of Brooklyn College's Scandinavian Cultural Society. New discoveries lay in wait—openings, now, not just to Northern Europe but also to unknown corners of New York—my hometown. I set foot, for the first time, on Staten Island—one of the five boroughs of New York City—thanks to Professor Samuel Abrahamsen, the academic advisor of the Scandinavian Cultural Society, originally from Norway, who made his U.S. home in Staten Island.

Sharing my experiences in Norway with the larger Brooklyn College community, I gave a presentation on what I had learned and my perceptions of the country. But this was just an initial step in informing the wider world about Norway, present and past.

Like a gift that keeps on giving, my Norwegian journey led me to the world of exhibition design and event planning. Whether thanks to a suggestion from Professor Abrahamsen, or a eureka moment of my own, I found myself organizing an exhibition on Norway for the Brooklyn College Library. We managed to involve the Royal Norwegian Consulate General in our undertaking, with the Consul General making a foray to Brooklyn to inaugurate the exhibition with his welcoming remarks. The exhibit was a successful event for the Scandinavian Cultural Society, with multiple pieces coming together and an informative display to pique the interest of students, faculty, and staff who might never have given the Nordic country a second thought.

In retrospect, my initial foray into cultural diplomacy was an extremely significant, formative building block in what would become many further ventures into cultural sharing. My cultural diplomacy path has led me to working with Visiting Senior Fulbright Scholars in the United States through the Council for International Exchange of Scholars, to organizing a multicultural festival in Waltham, Massachusetts, to enabling Burundian peacemakers to share their peace-building strategies with fellow peacemakers from Africa and elsewhere at the convening of the International Peace Research Association in Durban, South Africa. From Norway to the wider world, Brooklyn College and its Alumni Fund Summer Scholarship for Study Abroad opened the door.

Paul Goldberg, a Duke University graduate and now editor and publisher of The Cancer Letter, had this to say about his football glory:

Years after Duke, a friend told my two daughters the story of my humiliation in a football game between the second and third floors of the Gilbert-Addoms residence hall.

The friend, whom I call "the Bean," his actual nickname, recalled the story in graphic detail. He remembered the position I played: nose-guard. He was able to reconstruct the tackle in which I was sent flying. His punch line: Somebody forgot to tell me that I would be playing against an all-American high school player.

It's always a pleasure to regale the younger generation with stories of the stunts their parents pulled in their youth. But this story was different: I actually had nothing to hide. Indeed, I had heard that story before, in similarly graphic detail, with little variation. For a couple of years, it was part of the Gilbert-Addoms lore: how Boris (my nickname at the time) went splat on the football field.

Let me set the record straight. There was indeed a football game between the second and third floors of G-A that year. Though it was announced as "touch football," some players referred to it as "rip football" even before the game began. Some folks thought it would be amusing to have me play against an accomplished player. Yes, players on both teams suffered injuries. But I didn't play nose-guard. I wasn't on the field, or on the sidelines, or in the stands. I was elsewhere, probably in the library. If I were to risk my life and limb in pursuit of athletic glory, it would be in a sport I actually understood. Decades later, I still have no idea what happens on football fields.

I decided to embrace this account of my athletic humiliation, converting it into a series of bedtime stories for my daughters.

"After my talents were discovered in a dorm football game, I was recruited to play football for Duke," my story began. "They gave me a football scholarship and an orange Camaro. A cheerleader girlfriend soon followed. I didn't even have to go to classes anymore. One day, when we were playing Carolina, our arch-rival, I played nose-guard, my usual position, and the coach said, 'Goldberg, the quarterback has a terrible case of diarrhea, and we need you.'" Diarrhea got a laugh from the girls when they were younger, and, thankfully, it still does. In that story, I messed up a play and, in confusion, scored a touchdown for Carolina, and became an honorary captain of that team.

After that game, the Duke coach called me into his office and said, "Goldberg, Goldberg, Goldberg, what are we going to do with you?"

Granted, this story was further from what actually happened (or, in this case, didn't happen) than the one I heard recited by the Bean, but my daughters loved it, and, possibly, no harm was done.

The story of my football glory is still going strong. Even as adults, the girls frequently quote my coach's words of exasperation at my athletic ineptitude, and I fear that they will one day become my epitaph.

Museum expert Marsha Semmel made her way from the Detroit School of Arts to the first class of the University of Michigan's Residential College by taking risks and blurring boundaries:

In 1967, I was in the first class of the Residential College, an educational experiment at the University of Michigan that aimed to achieve small college intimacy within a Big Ten mega-university. There were 200 of us, approximately 100 men and 100 women who had checked the "yes" box on the application. The program's core curriculum focused on language mastery, logic and language, theme-based multidisciplinary courses in the humanities (exploring concepts such as salvation and covenant) and social sciences (looking at such big ideas as human development from different perspectives). The program featured small classes, mostly pass/fail, taught by senior faculty, and we students lived together in four of the ten houses within East Quadrangle.

My Detroit high school friends were puzzled: Why not simply enroll in the main liberal arts program or the Honors College, or choose a small college instead of the University of Michigan? Why take a chance on an experiment? How will you get into graduate school without a conventional transcript?

Why did I check that box? I didn't have the resources to attend a small private college; my options were limited to a public university. While I didn't consider myself a risk-taker, somehow the program appealed to my curious and creative self. Perhaps it was the fact that my downtown Detroit high school had more than 5,000 students—the Residential College's intimacy would be a welcome change. Perhaps it was the promise of more direct access to full professors.

I'm not sure about the why, but I do know that the experience turned out to be mind-expanding, lifetime-friend–making, challenging, and exhilarating. It was fun and exciting immersing myself in French, reading novels, writing papers, and engaging in conversations at the language-based lunch tables. And I never would have chosen a freshman seminar devoted to a semester-long analysis of Herodotus' *The Persian Wars*, with a renowned and demanding classics scholar; yet, that course yielded profound and lasting insights into historical interpretation, politics, and human nature. The cross-disciplinary explorations of humanities and social science themes introduced me to different approaches to knowledge (and knowledge creation) that have stayed with me throughout my career. I learned to analyze and critically compare ideas and defend my point of view. As our society continues to debate workplace needs, I'm continually reminded that the arts and the humanities provide the analytic and problem-solving perspectives that are at the heart of innovation and that attempt to address today's seemingly unsolvable challenges.

My Residential College experience stretched my brain, fueled my creativity, and gave me the tools and mindset to go both deep and broad. It helped stoke a lifelong hunger for learning and an appreciation of the complexity of human behavior. Without a doubt, it helped form the foundation for a gainful and rewarding career, as well as memorable experiences and encounters in the many decades since.

134

Something I Couldn't Have Done Before

Smith College librarian Sika Berger reflects on her first year as a student at Oberlin College and emphasizes the importance of developing confidence and building a personal comfort level in new environments:

In my first year at Oberlin, I enrolled in a challenging course with a few assertive, self-assured, and very vocal students. I was keenly interested in the topic, but contributing my thoughts to class discussions took something more than ordinary initiative.

Years after that class, I've seen this same scenario play out in my work with students at other colleges.

Had I spoken up in that thought-provoking class so early in my career at Oberlin, the professor and my classmates would have glimpsed my interests and views and the dominating few might have also learned the value of listening and learning from others.

I had not yet realized how valuable it is to be able to persevere and to build a level of comfort when the first impression of a new environment is so overwhelming.

What does it take to change course, to explore something outside your familiar way in the world? Habit enters into the equation. Curiosity, keeping your mind and senses open, building skills of observation, and taking some risks can all lead beyond the usual path.

My risk-taking opened new channels of communication and helped me to gain an understanding of other people's lives.

Despite my love of languages, I decided early on I wouldn't major in French or Spanish. Barely accustomed to a new place and a hectic schedule with classes, work, two radio shows, new friends, concerts, and more, I nevertheless gave what seemed like an absurd suggestion from my French professor some serious thought. By second semester, I was immersed in a foreign city, living with a family in France. As the program director's assistant, I gathered materials, prepared study sheets, and made reservations, visiting unknown parts of the country and meeting deadlines crucial to the success of the group's excursions.

We spent the last weeks of the semester in Paris, which made the previous months seem quite tame. I learned an alternate meaning for May Day, the international workers' holiday. I felt part of the international student community, explored sites both modern and historical, and ventured into the unknown—a cave party with plenty of wine, a local café, French movies, an enormous flea market, and the haunts of famous writers. The paper I wrote about French television was a challenge, but tied into my intended communication studies major. I will never regret the decision to load my first-year academic record with French credits through study abroad.

A January independent study project in Mexico brought another opportunity for finding new paths. Contributing to a professor's research, I interviewed women about the course of their lives, but I regret that I lacked the bravery to find more women in a broad range of professions. Risk-taking may also have its downside, as I learned while recovering from hepatitis after eating shellfish at a remote spot on the Pacific.

Exposure to documentary and feature films in college helped me to "read" them with different lenses. Creating and teaching others to produce film and video gave me a means of communicating ideas while encouraging others to do the same. Reading widely and keeping an open mind about people led by chance to friendship with a future Pulitzer Prize–winner and some understanding of the writer's craft.

Daring to audition for plays, even though I wasn't a theatre major, made me comfortable joining repertory and community theatre groups later on. My recent participation in a production of *The Voices of American Working People's History* grew out of several experiences. Witnessing the

French May Day, taking a labor history course, joining political rallies, producing programs for Radio Liberty, joining a union with my first job, and imparting to my children a love for many types of music all laid the groundwork for my involvement. I stepped up to join a multi-generational group in presenting the words of people who made a difference while drawing others in with songs. I'm not sure this would have been possible had I not developed the confidence many years ago to create my own path.

It Took a Little Courage

Anne Newsome graduated from Appalachian State University in 1998. She writes about a very personal experience that emanated from a class during her senior year:

During my senior year of college, I was taking a Human Relations and Interactions class. It was a small, interactive class that was very different from the typical lecture style of class. I loved my professor, Dr. Willie Fleming. He was caring and really great with students.

Dr. Fleming gave us a specific assignment that had to do with some type of a personal challenge. He asked us to conduct research and to then do a presentation on the personal challenge before the end of the semester. I remember feeling a lot of excitement about using this as a chance to do something I had always wanted to do.

I decided I was going to launch a search for my biological family. I had always known I would do this someday, and what better time than for this assignment?

I was two years old when I was adopted, and grew up knowing so. I hated not knowing anything for sure about a part of my life.

Of course, with something like this, you can never be sure how it will turn out, what you may find, or how you may end up feeling when all is said and done. There were definite ups and downs throughout the experience for me, and actually, it was just the beginning of what became an ongoing process of discovery and learning about my biological roots and my life for those two years.

Even though my adoption was closed, I was able to locate my birth family and my foster parents.

My foster parents came to Dr. Fleming's class for my presentation.

This reunion has affected my life tremendously, including helping me to better understand myself, to better complete the picture of my earliest life, and to see how the experience fits with who I am as a person today.

2009 Simmons College graduate Emily Slocum shares how the combination of New England winters and college internships led her to launch a clothing line:

I grew up in a small town called Castine, on the coast of Maine. I had five other kids in my elementary/middle school class, so deciding to move to Boston for college was quite a big step. I always knew I wanted to be in Boston, and Simmons College was attractive because it was a small but good school right in the middle of the city. Being all women, Simmons also had an empowering and somewhat fierce culture to it. This atmosphere was just what I needed in order to find my way as a soon-to-be young professional. I had several internships in college, including one in public relations at the Museum of Fine Arts.

The inspiration for my clothing line first came from trying to dress professionally as an intern.

Because I was a college student who had never stepped foot in an office, I had no idea what to wear to work. I went to Macy's and spent more money than I had on what I thought were the essentials: a few frumpy suits, a few oxford shirts that were too tight in the armpits but fit right everywhere else, a few pairs of pants that were too short, skirts that sat funny at the waist and would swivel from the back to the front after walking about thirty steps, and too many packages of itchy tights. Most of my new clothing was made with polyester and many fibers I had never heard of. Absolutely everything required dry cleaning.

I felt like a total adult when I wore my new clothes, but I was never quite comfortable in them. I could not wait to get back to my dorm room at the end of the day and change into yoga pants and a sweatshirt.

As the weather got colder (and if you have spent a winter in Boston you know what I am talking about), I found it to be impossible to both be prepared for the thirty-minute walk to my office and to look put-together when I got there.

At first, I just tried to brave it. I arrived at my office with wet shoes and paper-thin blouses, chilled to the bone with blue lips and fingers so frozen I could not hit the elevator numbers. After a week of that, I couldn't take it anymore. I put real Maine boots on my feet, sweatpants on over my tights, and a fleece on over my blouse and under my wool coat. I brought a huge bag with me with my stilettos and a blazer and as soon as I got off the elevator I would dash into the ladies room to sort out my outfit. It seemed ridiculous, but at the time it seemed to be the only way to go.

I realized this was not just a problem for me, and that other city girls also tortured themselves commuting to work. They, too, arrived half-frozen and then thawed out with space heaters, oversized scarves, and endless cups of hot tea throughout the morning. Even in the summer months, when the weather tables turn, the problem persists. It can be 90 degrees outside, so commutes aren't the difficult part of the day, but office air conditioning often plunges indoor temperatures to what feels like below-freezing conditions—and the space heaters, oversized scarves, and endless cups of hot tea become a year-round thing.

Being a girl nearing graduation and destined to spend an eternity wearing "career wear," I thought there had to be another way. Why should women have to freeze in order to dress professionally?

I decided to create my own clothing line in order to solve this problem. My product is a jacket that is super warm, extremely comfortable, and versatile enough to fit with just about any outfit a woman might wear in the office.

The jacket is also versatile enough to wear on the weekends, on the way to yoga, or over pajamas.

Thanks to my Maine upbringing, PR, marketing and advertising classes at Simmons College, and college internships in Boston, I have been able to help other professional women solve the battle of dressing warmly and comfortably while still looking great in the office.

Iona College graduate Louis Ferro shares how he failed to read the entirety of a rejection letter. It all turned out for the best, though:

While a student at Iona College, a small liberal arts school in Westchester County, New York, I decided to join the staff of our school newspaper. I worked on a number of stories for *The Ionian*, covering a range of topics from a local cat getting stuck in a tree to our school sports teams. After a couple of semesters, I was asked to be one of the associate editors.

I decided to push the envelope, if you will, by suggesting more creative and topical issues that affected not only our college community but the greater New York metropolitan area as well, including political campaigns and major cultural events.

We tried covering several political campaigns, but were rebuffed in our efforts. Political candidates, government entities, and large local companies really didn't take *The Ionian* and its band of college journalists very seriously. I spent considerable time brainstorming other possible stories and interviews to pursue.

As an avid baseball fan and a student journalist, I decided to write the New York Mets and ask for an interview with two of their star players. I sent off a letter to their public relations director and waited for the certain rejection.

After several weeks, the letter I expected did in fact arrive. Given the demand for interviews and the team's recent success, they said they would have to decline my request. I totally expected it. I stared at the letter and put it down. As quickly as I did, one of my colleagues picked it up, read it, and yelled out some expletives. But the expletives were laced with happiness.

In my disappointment, I failed to read the bottom of the letter wherein the team offered me two tickets and one press pass for every home stand during the season. What I thought was going to be a big letdown actually turned out to be an unexpected success. I covered the Mets as a beat reporter for the entire season and interacted with many of my favorite players.

I smile when I think about the whole experience, which taught me to carefully read letters, and to keep dreaming big.

Joan Nathan is the author of ten cookbooks, including Quiches, Kugels, and Couscous: My Search for Jewish Cooking in France. *She has won both the James Beard Award for the best American cookbook and the IACP/Julia Child Cookbook of the Year Award. Joan reflects on her University of Michigan days and her junior year abroad in Paris:*

When I started college at the University of Michigan in the early '70s, I was clueless about many aspects of life but knew that a lot of life revolved around food. I remember the dreary vegetarian co-op at the time in Ann Arbor that served brown rice and yogurt. The food was depressing, but at least it was pure. At my sorority house (Sigma Delta Tau), on the other hand, everything was processed—but we did love Mrs. Moyer's pies, and somehow feasted late at night on peanut butter and jelly.

Then I went to Paris for my junior year abroad. Everything changed. Not that I could afford great food, but I would try all the food I could from boudin blanc at student cafeterias at the Sorbonne, to Friday night dinners where the challah was a baguette. I was invited to taste Russian blini and caviar at a Russian émigré's restaurant, and went with a

French friend on a week of feasting at restaurants in Normandy where we tasted every regional specialty. My year in France shaped what I would do for the rest of my life: write about culture, history, and food. And I am still struggling with all those calories!

Janet Knaphle Loewe, former Director of Nursing Education at Clarks Summit State Hospital, shares a funny story from her time at the University of Cincinnati:

One of the most hilarious experiences during my student nursing days took place on a medical ward of Cincinnati General Hospital. At that time, it was a pavilion-designed structure, and the medical pavilion was made up of six separate wards, each one with its own laundry chute emptying into a large room in the basement.

I had completed the morning care of a male patient and disposed of his soiled hospital gown down the chute. Unfortunately, he had pinned a religious medal on to his gown and was quite upset when he realized it was missing.

The medal had to be retrieved. I made my way to the basement laundry room, but was confronted with the mystery of which of the many piles of soiled laundry belonged to my ward. In an effort to be of assistance, a classmate of mine stood over the ward's chute opening and began to shout my name. At that point, the head nurse, who also graded us on our performance, happened to arrive. She quickly surveyed the scene and concluded that I had fallen down the chute and ended up in a pile of dirty laundry. She didn't think it was nearly as funny as the rest of the hospital staff, my classmates, and everyone else who heard about it. To make matters worse, I never ended up finding the gown with the medal.

The story about the search for the soiled gown followed me for the rest of my student career.

Moving from laundry chutes in Cincinnati, Ohio, to cafeteria dumpsters in Des Moines, Iowa, Janelle Bartlett Mummey shares a story from her student days in the '90s at Drake University:

My freshman year, I had a really bad cold that required me to take Benadryl, which makes me incredibly sleepy and a little loopy. I had just been on a job interview and had my Drake ID, my social security card, and an "emergency" credit card that my mom had given me, all in a wallet holder that was attached to my room key. I went from class to lunch and then back to my room to take a nap. When I woke up later that afternoon, I couldn't find my wallet holder anywhere. The only thing that I could think of was that, in my Benadryl stupor, I must have thrown everything out with the rest of the contents on my food tray.

I was panicked! I was especially nervous to cancel the credit card, as my parents were on vacation and I didn't want to bother them or get my dad upset with my mom for lending me the card in the first place.

My roommate and some other girls from my floor decided to take pity on me and helped me look. The catch: The only place to look for my lost items was in the cafeteria's dumpster containing that day's garbage. My friends were so amazing. We all got in our grubbiest clothes and headed out that night to look. We searched through an entire dumpster full of discarded grilled cheese sandwiches and tomato soup, bag by bag, and found nothing. We were all dejected, tired, and gross as we headed back to the dorm.

When we got back to the dorm, our resident advisor told us to put our smelly clothes in the hall, and she collected them and washed them all for us. Everyone told me that I should just get some sleep and deal with everything in the morning.

I climbed into my loft bed and put my arms around my pillow. Lo and behold, underneath my pillow was the wallet holder we had all been looking for! I must have had it in my hand when I took the nap earlier.

My roommate was not amused. Neither were my other friends from my floor. Anyway, we all laugh about it now. What I realized is that these girls, whom I had only known a few short months, had my back. I knew that we had a special bond—which still exists today.

Rachel Guerrero, a 2012 graduate of Calvin College, teaches English as a Second Language in China. How she got to China is an interesting story:

I went into college freshman year as a declared Business major and Mandarin Chinese minor. The initial idea was that being able to speak Chinese would help my résumé look good to companies that did business in Asia. Even back then, I had a bit of a hard time picturing myself designing spreadsheets and making deals. I couldn't really envision myself doing the sort of job I was going to school for, but I didn't have any better ideas for a major, so that's what I went with.

I attended Chinese class on the very first day of first semester. That was the day I had my eyes opened to the world of Mandarin Chinese. My Chinese professor was an amazing teacher who would tell fascinating stories about the etymology of Chinese words so that it was nearly impossible to forget new vocabulary. He used props like puppets and toy cars to make class fun, but, more importantly, his passion for the language was contagious. I caught it. By the end of first semester, I had chosen not to proceed as a Business major and had instead become a Mandarin Chinese major.

I went on to take classes in Japanese. From there, I moved to Spanish. I was gradually learning that, while Mandarin Chinese was my first love when it came to foreign languages, I was fascinated by many of them. More than that, I was fascinated by the strategies used to teach languages in all of my classes. I began volunteering in an ESL (English as a Second Language) tutoring program that was organized by my college. Shortly before I graduated, my college began offering an ESL minor, one that fascinated me immensely, but, alas, it was too late for me to both add that minor and graduate on schedule.

Many people asked me what I was going to do with my major in Mandarin Chinese, and, I'll admit, at first I didn't really know. I considered a few different tracks of grad school: Asian Studies? Linguistics? But I wasn't willing to commit the time, money, and energy to a grad school program that I wasn't completely sure about.

Some time after graduation, my husband and I nearly simultaneously began to consider the thought of moving abroad to work. My younger sister mentioned to me that several of her friends had moved to South Korea to teach English. I wondered whether China had similar opportunities for teaching English, since, at least in China, I'd speak the local language.

As it turns out, China indeed has countless jobs available for people who can teach, and my husband and I both ended up in careers that we had never even considered at the start of college: We're ESL teachers. Every time I walk into my classroom, I'm reminded how much I love my job. I think I know now why I found that very first Mandarin Chinese class so fascinating. My professor was doing exactly what I wanted to do for a living, but I just didn't know it yet. I use my degree on a daily basis. I use the language in everyday conversations, and I use the best language-teaching strategies I observed in college in teaching my own classes.

Peggy Printz, former editor and publisher of Study in the USA, reflects on her time at Smith College during the escalation of conflict in Vietnam:

It wasn't my Smith College junior year abroad that eventually led to my career as the publisher of magazines and websites for international students. It wasn't the rigorous Smith emphasis on analytical writing. It wasn't even the challenge of having classmates who became outstanding peers of my generation.

All of those experiences provided catalytic material for my rewarding career. But if I had to choose one incident that propelled me to a life of leadership, it would be the student anti-war protest that occurred during Smith commencement in 1967.

Attorney General Nicholas Katzenbach was set to be our speaker. He represented the Johnson Administration, which in those years was escalating the conflict in Vietnam. Until that spring, I had marched in only one demonstration, on a weekend trip to New York City, and that half-heartedly because my friends were more interested in people-watching than in actually reaching the United Nations building. That memory was shameful to me, but I didn't know how to express my anger against the war within my own personal context, living on campus in rural Massachusetts.

I hadn't been eligible to vote, as I only attained the pre-1971 voting age of 21 after the 1966 election. It was only in subsequent years that university students began participating more vociferously in electoral campaigns.

Then the opportunity arose: A group of acquaintances in my senior class were planning to demonstrate during our commencement ceremony against Attorney General Katzenbach and government policies. Our action would be peaceful but provocative. We would wear white armbands over our black robes. We would leave printed flyers expressing our sentiments on the chairs so everyone in the audience would be aware of our effort.

Because I planned to enter the field of journalism, I went to the first meeting and offered to help draft the statement. Gradually taking more of a leadership role, I relished the opportunity. I grew comfortable initiating ideas and working with other class leaders. Collaborating with them, I found my public voice. Ever after, I have readily found the courage to express dissenting opinions and to take charge in sensitive situations.

I hope my contributions resulted in a more effective statement.

Only a minority of my classmates joined the protest, but today, we remember it as a major event of our college careers. It is also a potent marker of the upheavals that were then overhauling U.S. education, as campuses became focal points for activism and engagement with the community.

Our protest even inspired some faculty members to prepare their own petition.

You can still find excerpts from our flyer online:

"We the undersigned graduating seniors of Smith College take this opportunity to express our opposition to our government's responsibility for widening the conflict in Vietnam ... Our dissent is born of patriotism. It is because we care that we protest."

Nancy Donaldson is director of the International Labor Organization's Washington office. She reflects on resilience and her college years at Baldwin Wallace College, now Baldwin Wallace University:

In the summer of 1972, I gave up my plan to leave the United States (a stand against the Watergate scandal) and enrolled as a freshman at Baldwin Wallace in Berea, Ohio. From the beginning, and throughout my time in college, I was a commuter student, focused on counseling urban teens in my free time. I decided to study Persian poetry, physics, the Gnostic Gospels, and sociology. I had an early windfall gaining the support of two mentors on the faculty. No one dissuaded me from the idea that college was for learning and experiments, and that course design and curricula could be imagined into being. I received permission to design my own major.

I pursued "independent studies" and taught a course on creativity at a local high school. I gave the students an assignment to follow a homeless person and observe how they manage their days. It drew attention from the authorities, but I wasn't thrown out. I co-taught semantics with my professor, Dan Kirk, and fell in love with the works of linguist S. I. Hayakawa.

By the time I graduated, I had accumulated more than a year of credits for off-campus learning. This included enrollment in full-time training in the theory and application of Gestalt psychology at the Gestalt Institute of Cleveland. In the summer of 1974, I gave up my VW bug with the "Impeach Nixon" bumper sticker, and moved to Koinonia Farm in Sumter County, Georgia. For 3 months, I lived and worked in one of the oldest communes in the United States. I worked in their small factory employing locals, pressing polyester pants, and listening to tapes by the spiritual writer Thomas Merton. Living at Koinonia was part of my opportunity in college to think seriously about what I wanted to do with my life. When I returned home to Cleveland, my father was greatly relieved that I came back at all. I took pleasure in surprising him by announcing that I wanted to go to law school.

In my senior year at Baldwin Wallace, I worked as volunteer staff for the Seventh Step Foundation, an NGO founded and run by prisoners and ex-cons. When the director was arrested for embezzling funds, I wrote about how things can fall apart. I studied human systems, organizational psychology, and the role of communication in accomplishments and failures in human enterprises. I called my major "Interpersonal Communications."

Before graduating, I organized an oral presentation to share some of my college learning with professors, family, and friends. For me, it was an important exercise: It never crossed my mind that it might be anything but interesting for others. The registrar told me later that he was relieved to see me go.

During the last week of school, I met with my professors to receive their observations and wisdom before graduating with honors and heading to Emory University Law School. They gave me plenty to think about. The most memorable advice came in three words: remember your resilience.

Carol Olmstead, now a Feng Shui Master Practitioner, shares a story from a college internship that taught her to not be afraid of unorthodox decisions:

In the summer of my junior year as a journalism major at the University of Maryland, College Park, I won a coveted spot in the Magazine Publishers Association college intern program. There were thirty of us from across the country, each assigned to magazines in New York City. The participating publications included *Newsweek, Time,* and what for me would have been the prize assignment, *The New Yorker.* What did I get? *Woman's Day Magazine.* It was 1970 and I couldn't believe I had to work for a "housewife" magazine that featured articles like making your child's Halloween mask from a plastic bleach container. Yes, that was not only an actual article, but one that I wrote that summer as well.

The first day I walked into their editorial offices, I was surprised to find that I had entered a hotbed of feminism. The staff was young and hip, rather than the stuffy group of "old ladies" I had expected to find. I ended up loving every minute of the five weeks I worked there. I especially remember a phone conversation with the Princess of Monaco to set up an interview with one of the editors:

"Hello, this is Grace Kelly," she said in her regal voice when I answered what I thought would be a typical phone conversation.

And the surprises kept coming.

Toward the end of my internship, Editor Geraldine Rhoads took me to a publishers' luncheon in a private club on Madison Avenue. When we checked in, the receptionist said that we had to enter the dining room through the kitchen. After all, this was an all-male club.

"I will not go through the kitchen," Geraldine replied.

She grabbed my hand and with head held high she marched us through the library into the dining room. A few men looked up and scowled, but most didn't even notice. We sat down at our table, and my heart was pounding.

"Did we just do that?" my old naive self asked. "We just did that!" my new, more self-assured self replied.

My world was forever changed as I realized I didn't have to follow what was expected of me and that I could make decisions that were outside the box, no matter how odd.

Teresa Temkin, a 2011 graduate of Vanderbilt University, explains how a course about Grimm's Fairy Tales helped her to be open to new experiences:

A skill that I learned in college was to be open to new experiences and to be willing to seize opportunities. This has been vital to my career.

At Vanderbilt, I realized that I had a whole world of information at my fingertips. There, like at many colleges, classes had to be taken that filled certain requirements. One such requirement could be filled by any number of classes that ranged in topics from English 101 to Grimm's Fairy Tales. Though each class would have been worth the same credit on my final transcript, the experience gained by taking the Grimm's Fairy Tales class was ultimately more enriching. By acting on the opportunity to enrich my own experiences, I was better served than had I just taken a "normal" course of study. College taught me that the chances existed and that I just had to find them.

It was after graduation, when I was still figuring out what to do, that I spoke to my childhood librarian. She suggested that I look into pursuing a degree in Library Science. Again, I took that chance, that opportunity, and ended up applying to and then attending Florida State University's School of Information.

For a long time, my desire has been for a career path that would allow me to keep reading and learning in the long term. To that end, my time at FSU granted me three amazing internship opportunities. The first of these was to work with the State Department at the U.S. Mission to NATO in Brussels, Belgium. The second took me to College Station, Texas, where I worked with both the textual and audiovisual archival records departments at the George Bush Presidential Library and Museum. My third internship was with the State Department in Washington, D.C. Each of these internships was extremely different in terms of tasks and experiences, yet they all drew from the skills and education I received in the pursuit of my Library Science degree. Even more pointedly, none of them would have been possible had I not been willing to seize the opportunities presented to me.

Friendship and Camaraderie

Fern Fleischer Daves, an attorney in New York, reflects on how connecting with someone from her freshman year dorm at American University led to a lifelong friendship:

You just never know. Someone you meet on the first day of college may become your lifelong friend.

When I was 17, I just couldn't wait to get far enough away from Miami Beach to start my life at college. I arrived in Washington, D.C., never having been there before, knowing absolutely no one. And that was okay with me.

I was so excited the first moment I walked through the beautiful tree-lined campus of American University. I found my dorm—and then paused. 1970s' ugly architecture, cinderblock walls, two beds, two dressers, and two desks were squeezed into an 8 x 12 room. There was a shared restrooms arrangement.

Little did I know that one of the three Susans among the twenty-four women on the first floor of Letts Hall would be my dear friend thirty years later.

This Susan and I didn't have much in common on that first day of college, except that we were both really happy to be far away from home, and we discovered that we both really liked ice cream. We had vastly different backgrounds and interests. We never took a class together, but we did have a lot of fun and a great connection.

Susan grew up in Bay Ridge, Brooklyn, a middle-class, Italian-American neighborhood full of extended families living in two-family row houses with grandparents, cousins, great aunts, and friends that extended across three generations. Susan excelled at the local Catholic school in academics and sports, and earned a basketball scholarship to American. Susan's family was warm and generous, and the kitchen shared by her mother and grandmother was always full of delicious and ready-to-eat delicacies. Susan's dad could fix anything, and he provided a gasoline station credit card so that we could come home any weekend during the school year. And we did that often enough that he was willing to drive us anywhere in the greater New York area so that we could completely avoid public transportation. I always felt safe and warm with her family. Susan liked so many things—and was good at so many of them—that she changed her major every other term.

I grew up mostly in Miami Beach where I went to the same public schools that my mother attended. I was a bit of a nerd, in the middle of the pack in the AP and honors courses, and my circle of friends were from the neighborhood and Jewish youth group. Like many of my friends, my parents divorced when I was in elementary school and my father was a once-a-year vacation-time dad who lived out of state with wife number two. My mom was busy with working, finishing college at night, and trying to have a social life while raising three kids. She didn't cook much, and didn't even notice when I "checked out" of 10th grade—rarely attending some classes, trying to flunk out of others. This was my completely ineffective attempt to get attention during a period of family crisis when my dad was diagnosed with cancer, and we were displaced from our home for several months after a fire.

If I hadn't pulled that ridiculous stunt, I might have earned a full scholarship to college. I bore the punishment well—going to summer school in the mornings and taking a community college math course. AU did provide some need-based financial aid, but I worked my way through college as I accumulated student debt. With Susan's encouragement and support, I earned top grades in all the courses I enjoyed. I graduated on time and added a fifth year on full scholarship for a master's degree.

Susan is still the person I call first when I need a little encouragement or a good laugh. We continue to share our lives with each other. Recently, she sent me a text with a picture from our first Halloween together at AU. She helped make my costume—and we still laugh about it to this day.

Another college story involving New York, more specifically Carnegie Hall and the Empire State Building, comes from attorney Enid Hurwitz Adler:

What happens when you combine the Philadelphia Orchestra, Temple University Choir, Carnegie Hall, Beethoven, and the Empire State Building? You get a funny story that I still remember.

My first trip to New York City occurred during my freshman year at Temple University. I was a music major (in voice) and I sang with the Temple University Choir. We were the choir of choice of Eugene Ormandy, conductor of the Philadelphia Orchestra. The weekend orchestra series in Philadelphia usually included a Tuesday night performance at New York City's Carnegie Hall. On that night, it was Beethoven's Ninth Symphony.

Between the late afternoon rehearsal and evening performance, my real adventure began.

I always wanted to see the Empire State Building. So I hopped on a 7th Avenue bus that would take me from Carnegie Hall at 57th Street down to 34th Street, where I found my way to my goal. Up I went in the Empire State Building elevator to the observation deck. The view was spectacular, and I was very happy that I made it by myself.

Mission accomplished, but not yet over.

Now I had to figure out how to get back uptown. 7th Avenue was one-way going downtown, so I couldn't take that bus—and I certainly didn't have enough money for a taxi.

Fortunately, I met some friendly locals who pointed me in the direction of an uptown bus.

I was a bit late getting back to Carnegie Hall, but I am proud to say that I made it.

At first, my friends were sure that I had gotten swallowed up. And they were relieved to see me when I made it back. In my honor, they later presented me with an oversized postcard of the Empire State Building that was signed by my choir mates.

Kirstin Barry is a 2010 graduate of the University of Rochester and associate director of Kappa Delta Sorority, a national sorority with more than 200,000 members. She shares an experience that makes her laugh and demonstrates how people can have an impact on your life in unexpected ways:

As a high school senior, I visited the University of Rochester and had a fantastic visit with a junior student tour guide named Jason. Jason was super involved on campus and gave my mom and me such a pleasant experience, eating lunch with us in the dining hall, taking us on a tour, and talking openly and honestly about his experience.

Upon arriving at the University of Rochester freshman year, I quickly learned that being a tour guide, called a meridian at Rochester, was one of the most prestigious positions on campus. The application process was rigorous, as only the best and brightest students got chosen—about twenty new tour guides each year out of hundreds of applicants. I submitted my application, hoping to advance to the next round—to make a presentation in front of the entire applicant group and selection committee.

I was devastated to receive an email that I was not selected to advance.

A few weeks later, as I helped some girls on my freshman hall prepare for the presentation round before the interview, I received an email from the director of meridians saying that he had received an anonymous recommendation about me and would like to invite me to the interview round.

An anonymous recommendation about me? I had only been at school for a few months. How did this happen? Dismissing these questions and eagerly accepting the opportunity, I prepared for the interview, and landed the job! Who was that anonymous recommender? I guessed I would never know.

Months later, during sorority recruitment in January, I was sitting in the final recruitment round at the sorority chapter that I had fallen in love with. Two sisters I had gotten to know during the fall semester were talking to me about why they joined the sorority. They talked about the activities they'd gotten involved with at Rochester because of the sorority, which led me to tell them the unusual story about how I became a meridian.

Much to my surprise, one of the women talking to me, a senior named Lindsey, confessed that she was the one who gave the anonymous recommendation to the Admissions Office to bring me in for a meridian interview. She had talked to me very briefly a few times on campus. Even through these had been short interactions, she felt like I would do an exceptional job and should be given a second chance. I started to tear up, feeling so grateful for this woman, who acted on a first impression, and gave me a special opportunity.

The moral of the story is that you never know who you might meet and how those people can possibly affect your life. Be authentic and be kind, because even the faintest acquaintance could vouch for you and give you an opportunity that otherwise you wouldn't have.

Erin Owen is the owner of Waynesville Pilates studio and a ballet and modern dance teacher. She graduated from Scripps College in 1999 and credits her college roommate with persuading her to attend an early morning audition that turned out to be pivotal:

I majored in dance and biology at Scripps College, and in my senior year, I had a hard time deciding which field I wanted to actively pursue. I landed on dance, figuring that I could go to graduate school later for biology if a career in dance didn't work out. I was leaning heavily toward staying on the West Coast. San Francisco had a modest but decent contemporary dance scene at the time, and I loved being in California. But then I saw a flyer for scholarship auditions to the Martha Graham School in New York City. I made plans to audition, not because I thought I would win a scholarship, but as practice. I wanted to begin acclimating myself to that process, foreseeing future dance auditions to gain employment as a professional.

During the final semester of my senior year, I was pretty overcommitted. I was trying to fit everything I possibly could, both academic and social, into those last precious months of college. Somewhere between writing my thesis and choreographing my final dance project, I forgot to register for the audition. The registration deadline had passed, and I was upset with myself for dropping the ball.

The weekend of the audition arrived, and I was exhausted. I was looking forward to sleeping in that Saturday morning, but my roommate (and to this day, dear friend) woke me up and announced that she was taking me to the audition. I told her it was too late and that there was no way they would let me in. But my whiny, sleep-deprived complaints fell on deaf (smart, brave) ears. She was ready to go. With my eyes half closed, I grabbed a leotard and tights and off we went.

They did let me in. Good grief, I did win a scholarship. It brought me to New York. One thing led to another and I lived and worked in New York for sixteen years as a professional dancer. I had a very full career, performing and teaching globally with some of my favorite dance artists.

This was all because of my caring and motivated friend, who orchestrated a twist of fate that Saturday morning.

Kari Comer, a 2015 graduate of the University of Alabama, is a speech-language pathologist. She writes about her feeling part of the campus community:

My favorite memory from college is the feeling of being part of something amazing!

From the first moment I stepped foot on campus at the University of Alabama, I felt like I had the world at my fingertips. I was overwhelmed by the excitement of the possibilities: friends to be made, parties to attend, football games, and choosing a major.

My freshman year seemed chaotic with me trying to decide what I wanted to study. I tried a lot on for size, but I finally decided just before my sophomore year: my chosen major was Communicative Disorders with a minor in Human Development.

Just like my love for the campus, my love for speech-language pathology was instantaneous. It seemed like the perfect amalgamation of my interests in language, cognition, and behavior. The program was small, but the cohort became family quickly, and the majority of us stayed on for graduate school.

My time was regularly spent in class, studying, or at the Wesley Methodist Student Foundation. The people I met in class and church became my closest friends. We went out several nights a week, starting with dinner and happy hour, then danced the night away to music played by some of our local favorite bands. Sleep wasn't a priority, so we were still able to get to class on time at 8 a.m. the next morning and find time to study afterward.

Game day weekends were even more exciting. One of my favorite T-shirts did a great job of capturing the feeling: "Watching football with 100,000 of your closest friends."

You felt like you knew everyone by their friendly waves and the Roll Tide rally cry. The energy and excitement was intoxicating!

Elizabeth Miller, a graduate of the University of Iowa, also shares what it felt like to be part of a campus community that supports a Division I football team:

Everybody was there—and by everybody, I mean 70,585 Iowans from all walks of life! The Ph.D. students, the law students, the religion students, the fraternity and sorority students, the professors, the administration, the president, the governor, and half the state of Iowa. Everybody was decked out in black and gold. It was about Iowa Hawkeye football, for sure, but when I think back on it, it was also about being a part of a larger community.

Those fall Saturdays started out warm and humid in September, and by the last home game, we were sitting in parkas in the snow. Our enthusiasm remained strong and unwavering. In cheering and supporting our school, the bonds of friendship and connection with friends sitting on my right and left always grew stronger.

I think back on those moments as times that helped me understand the world around me, when I developed relationships and lasting bonds with the people and a place that remain important in my life to this day.

So what was it like? The walk from the dormitories on campus to the stadium on the far side of campus is one to behold. I remember taking my husband to a game for the first time, and his mouth hung to the ground. He was speechless as he tried to absorb the spectacle of it all.

Fans of all ages walk en masse toward the Kinnick gates that somewhat resemble the pearly gates—at least to those of us in Iowa. It is hard to find anyone who isn't wearing a Hawkeye logo somewhere on their person. Along the way, there are multiple places to stop and enjoy refreshments of all kinds.

It's loud. It's rowdy. It's somewhat unsettling in a good way. And all the while you can hear the band playing and the crowd cheering inside that stadium. It's a pull like none other.

Walking inside Kinnick Stadium is transformational for almost everyone. The sensory overload is unparalleled from the moment you step through the gates until the game is over. Iowa's marching band is legendary. The fans love the halftime show nearly as much as the game itself.

I remember laughing and cheering and building camaraderie with my fellow students and Iowans. It's not all about the books and the intellectual growth—have some fun and make lasting friendships along the way. You may end up learning more than you realize.

Cultural media producer and writer William Gilcher reflects on his background and his time at Hamilton College in Clinton, New York. His transition from one type of economic community to another captures a phenomenon that can be difficult for many to acknowledge:

Coming from a working-class family and landing at a small and tweedy college, I wish I had had an advisor or teacher who recognized the cultural gap between young men like me and the majority of the students. Certainly, I was not the only one in this situation, and I found friends of all social classes at Hamilton, but I didn't really remember anyone who talked openly about this kind of issue. Perhaps we didn't (and still don't) realize that there were (and are) social classes in the United States.

Afterword

William's point is well taken—and is a good place to end this book.

In your quest for an educational institution that fits you, don't forget to take into account all the factors that could influence your future learning experiences. Look at your academic, intellectual, social, and extracurricular background. Think seriously about the type of student that you are and that you hope to be in the future. Reflect on the activities you plan to continue doing in college and those that you might like to do for the first time. Think seriously about your willingness to go beyond where you came from.

Hopefully, you'll take the stories you just read and apply lessons from them to your own life. How can you combine classroom and extracurricular learning in ways that will help you during college and afterward? What subjects and activities excite you the most? What types of learning communities most appeal to the way you hope to grow?

As you evaluate various colleges and universities, as well as specific programs within different colleges, I urge you to explore many paths that might become available. Watch for opportunities that are presented to you as well as those you can create.

When the search is over and you are a matriculated college student, don't be afraid to continue challenging yourself and reaching as high as you can. It's natural to have some fear of failure, but in my view, you should be more afraid of not trying. Consider this book as permission to give things the proverbial "college try" that both you and society deserve.

Acknowledgments

Thank you to the following contributors:

Tough Choices
Roy Pomerantz, Columbia University
Jerome Hill, Syracuse University
Danny Ly, Portland State University
Stephanie Seibel, Sonoma State University
Margaret King, University of Oregon

Good Advice
Samantha Auburn Levine, Skidmore College
Carl Ehrlich, Harvard University
Ed Lazere, Harvard University
Rachelle Jailer Valladares, American University
Gwen Cummings, University of Oregon
Jon Clemmons, North Carolina State University
Evelyn Pereira, The College of New Jersey

I Didn't Give Up
Monika Blaumueller, Michigan State University
Julia Karpeisky, University of Kentucky
Katherine Vogel Anderson, Florida State University
Jennifer Laszlo Mizrahi, Emory University
Mark S., University of Virginia
Carol Christen, UCLA

Solving Problems
Kiki Skagen Munshi, Swarthmore College
Emily L., Carnegie Mellon University
Dr. Robert Wald, Washington University School of
  Medicine in St. Louis

Roland Machold, Yale University
Edie Maddy-Weitzman, Brandeis University

Mistakes Revisited
Robert Tomkin, University of New Hampshire
Gordon Rooney, University of Texas
Bill Caldwell, University of Georgia
Trooper Sanders, University of Michigan and the
    London School of Economics
Pete McCall, University of Tennessee at Chattanooga

Learning to Adapt
Jonathan Blyth, Franklin & Marshall College
Edward Dunar, Yale University
Liz Droge-Young, Colorado State University
Terence Fernando, University of Pennsylvania Law
    School
Marc Landis, Princeton University
Darshan Somashekar, Brown University
Tom Sansone, Boston University
Ambassador Richard Kauzlarich, Black Hawk College
Jim Gelb, Harvard University
Anne Arnold, University of Michigan
Rebecca Chura, University of Miami
Andrew Rothschild, Northwestern University
Mindy Kay Smith, Ohio University

Opening My Mind
Dr. Aaron Kesselheim, Harvard University
Scott Breen, Georgetown University
Dr. James C. Goodloe IV, Davidson College
Joseph Coci, University of Virginia
Laura Hendricks, Ohio University
Matt F., University of Dallas
Stephanie Scherpf, University of Virginia
Chris Svoboda, Sweet Briar College

Acknowledgments

Jeff Spicher, Eastern Mennonite University

The Unexpected
Dode Levenson, University of Massachusetts Amherst
James Minichello, University of South Carolina
Karen Rindge, University of North Carolina
Sandeep Seth, University of Texas
Dr. Linda Scherr, Cornell University
Nick Noble, Trinity College
Phil Rosenthal, University of Chicago
Nura Sadeghpour, University of California, Berkeley
Shelly Beaser, Temple University
Peter Waldheim, University of Wisconsin-Milwaukee
Clay Eals, University of Oregon
Dr. Scott Berkenblit, MIT
Matthew Weissman, Brown University

A Teacher or Mentor Who Changed My Life
Eddy Friedfeld, Columbia University
Tad Daley, Knox College
Dr. Ed Gomes, Liberty University
Cathleen Hanson, Towson University
Jennifer K., Boston University
Kristina Korsholm, UCLA
Katherine Dayton, Dickinson College
Tiffany Harris, Seattle University
Bruce Dehnert, Alfred University
Dr. Joy Dubost, Hood College
Debra Polsky, Rhodes College
Kiara Ana Perico, Boston University
Bruce Payne, University of California, Berkeley

Something I Couldn't Have Done Before
Charla Bailey, Emporia State University
Dr. Mindy Reiser, Brooklyn College
Paul Goldberg, Duke University

Marsha Semmel, University of Michigan
Sika Berger, Oberlin College

It Took a Little Courage
Anne Newsome, Appalachian State University
Emily Slocum, Simmons College
Louis Ferro, Iona College
Joan Nathan, University of Michigan
Janet Knaphle Loewe, University of Cincinnati
Janelle Bartlett Mummey, Drake University
Rachel Guerrero, Calvin College
Peggy Printz, Smith College
Nancy Donaldson, Baldwin Wallace University
Carol Olmstead, University of Maryland, College Park
Teresa Temkin, Vanderbilt University

Friendship and Camaraderie
Fern Fleischer Daves, American University
Enid Hurwitz Adler, Temple University
Kirstin Barry, University of Rochester
Erin Owen, Scripps College
Kari Comer, University of Alabama
Elizabeth Miller, University of Iowa
William Gilcher, Hamilton College

Special thanks to my wife, Jennifer Luray, and daughter, Mia Goodman, both of whom shared insightful perspectives on the college stories in this book.

Special thanks to Carol Nicotera-Ward for her good humor and guidance.

Special thanks also to university communities in the United States and around the world that have contributed to my deeper understanding of higher education.

Steven Roy Goodman is an international authority on college and graduate school admissions. In addition to his two books, Steve hosts a long-running television talk show about higher education issues. He has designed admissions strategies for more than 1,800 applicants to colleges, graduate programs, and business, law, and medical schools.

Miniver Press publishes lively and informative non-fiction books with a special focus on history and culture. For more information see http://www.miniverpress.com

Made in the USA
Columbia, SC
01 February 2018